The Good Food Guide Dinner Party Book

recipes from restaurants in The Good Food Guide
cooked, written, arranged and introduced by

HILARY FAWCETT AND JEANNE STRANG

CONSUMERS' ASSOCIATION

HODDER AND STOUGHTON

The Good Food Guide Dinner Party Book
published in Great Britain by
Consumers' Association,
14 Buckingham Street, London WC2N 6DS and
Hodder and Stoughton Ltd,
Mill Road, Dunton Green, Sevenoaks, Kent

First published in November 1971
Second impression December 1971
Third impression with minor amendments August 1975
Fourth impression March 1977
Fifth impression April 1979

ISBN 0 340 15790 8

Illustrations by Mart Kempers
Design by Banks & Miles
Printed and bound in Great Britain by
Butler and Tanner Ltd,
Frome, Somerset

Contents

Cost is a rough-and-ready guide to the comparative expense of dishes within the same category (first course, main dish, sweet, vegetable, bread). Obviously it will vary as specific ingredients rise or fall in price. The fewer the symbols, the less the cost.

Effort covers the duration and difficulty of work in the kitchen, not shopping, and must vary with the individual reader's temperament and cooking skills. These suggestions reflect our own experience in 'cooking' the book. The fewer the symbols, the less the effort.

PAGE		COST	EFFORT
7	Foreword		
10	Introduction		
18	**Spring menu 1**		
20	almond and watercress soup *or*	◎	▣▣
	tuna and corn bisque	◎	▣▣
21	chicken de Vaux	◎◎	▣▣
22	Sailors' Lament *or*	◎◎	▣▣▣
	chocolate brandy cake	◎◎◎	▣
23	**Spring menu 2**		
25	asparagus flan *or*	◎◎	▣▣
	onion cream tart	◎◎	▣▣
26	stuffed shoulder of veal, paysanne	◎◎	▣▣▣
27	kishmish *or*	◎◎	▣
	mousse au chocolat	◎◎	▣▣
28	**Spring menu 3**		
30	spiced spare ribs *or*	◎◎	▣▣
	spare ribs in honey	◎◎	▣▣

PAGE		COST	EFFORT
31	turbot kebabs with shrimp sauce	◎◎◎	▣▣
32	orange caramel trifle	◎◎◎	▣▣
33	**Spring menu 4**		
35	pignatelle	◎	▣▣
36	braised beef in red wine, cabbage with onion	◎◎	▣▣
37	brown bread ice-cream *or*	◎◎	▣
	caramel ice-cream	◎◎	▣
38	**Spring menu 5**		
40	avocado mousse *or*	◎◎◎	▣▣
	smoked trout pâté	◎◎◎	▣
41	liver with Dubonnet and orange	◎◎	▣
42	gateau Fontes *or*	◎◎◎	▣
	Lockets savoury	◎◎	▣
43	**Spring menu 6**		
45	terrine de campagne *or*	◎◎	▣▣
	oeufs Belle Anna	◎◎	▣
46	agnello e patate alla Villa Cesare	◎◎◎	▣▣▣
47	spiced pears	◎◎	▣
48	**Spring menu 7**		
49	pigeon casserole with celery and walnuts	◎◎	▣▣
	red cabbage	◎	▣
50	orange and lemon charlotte	◎◎◎	▣▣▣
52	**Summer menu 1**		
54	chachouka *or*	◎◎	▣
	ratatouille	◎◎	▣
55	involtini alla casareccia	◎◎◎	▣▣

PAGE		COST	EFFORT
56	strawberry pots de crème *or*	◎◎◎	▨▨
	fraises Charles Stuart	◎◎◎	▨
57	**Summer menu 2**		
59	fresh grapefruit and crab salad *or*	◎◎◎	▨▨
	salade niçoise	◎◎	▨
60	steak à la moutarde *or*	◎◎◎	▨
	tournedos Médicis	◎◎◎	▨
61	apricot torte with almonds	◎◎◎	▨▨▨
62	**Summer menu 3**		
64	smoked haddock croquettes *or*	◎◎	▨▨▨
	gazpacho	◎	▨▨
65	caneton aux olives	◎◎◎	▨▨
66	raspberry Pavlova *or*	◎◎◎	▨▨
	gooseberry meringue tart	◎	▨▨▨
67	**Summer menu 4**		
69	prawn cocktail *or*	◎◎◎	▨▨
	crab mousse	◎◎	▨▨
70	coeur de filet de porc aux herbes	◎	▨
	tomates provençale	◎	▨
71	ambroisie de pêches *or*	◎◎	▨
	blackcurrant ice-cream	◎◎	▨
72	**Summer menu 5**		
74	tortilla mimosa *or*	◎◎	▨
	omelette Arnold Bennett	◎◎	▨▨
75	fasulya, jeryik	◎◎	▨
76	Mrs Langan's chocolate pudding	◎◎◎	▨▨▨
77	**Summer menu 6**		
79	lemon soup *or*	◎◎	▨▨
	cold curried apple soup	◎	▨▨
80	darne de saumon de Médicis	◎◎◎	▨▨
81	American cheesecake *or*	◎◎	▨▨
	Italian cheesecake	◎◎	▨
82	**Summer menu 7**		
83	salmon pâté *or*	◎◎◎	▨
	Oak House pâté	◎◎	▨
84	American chicken salad	◎◎	▨▨
84	orange curd cream	◎◎	▨
86	**Autumn menu 1**		
88	Bell Inn smokies *or*	◎◎◎	▨
	marinated kipper fillets	◎	▨
89	steak and kidney pudding	◎	▨▨
90	marrow with curry sauce	◎	▨
90	apple and Stilton savoury	◎◎	▨
91	**Autumn menu 2**		
93	spinach soup *or*	◎	▨▨
	tomato soup	◎◎	▨▨
94	poulet au gratin à la crème landaise	◎◎◎	▨▨▨
95	tarte aux pommes Joséphine	◎	▨▨
96	**Autumn menu 3**		
98	Inwoods savoury pancakes *or*	◎◎	▨▨▨
	stuffed tomatoes	◎◎	▨
99	ris de veau au beurre noisette	◎◎	▨▨
	leeks in cream	◎	▨
100	Cold Love	◎◎◎	▨▨▨

PAGE		COST	EFFORT
101	**Autumn menu 4**		
103	chilled cream of mushroom soup *or*	◎◎	▣▣
	potage de garbanzos	◎	▣▣▣
162	roast duck	◎◎◎	▣
101	pureed potatoes and chestnuts	◎◎	▣
104	port and orange sauce *or*	◎◎◎	▣
	pickled pineapple *or*	◎◎	▣
105	prune and Beaujolais sauce	◎◎◎	▣
105	cherry and almond tart	◎◎◎	▣▣
106	**Autumn menu 5**		
108	Jaegermeister pâté with Waldorf salad	◎◎◎	▣▣
108	scampi façon Gourmet	◎◎◎	▣▣
109	chocolate cream with maraschino *or*	◎◎	▣▣
	crème velour	◎◎◎	▣▣
110	**Autumn menu 6**		
112	cream of cauliflower soup *or*	◎	▣▣
	scallop and artichoke soup	◎◎	▣▣
113	pork Basil Brush, rösti	◎	▣▣
114	hot fruit salad *or*	◎◎◎	▣▣
	peach Melba	◎◎	▣
115	**Autumn menu 7**		
117	sole Baie des Anges	◎	▣▣▣
118	apricot streusel	◎◎	▣▣▣
120	**Winter menu 1**		
122	moules marinière *or*	◎◎	▣▣▣
	mussels in cream and curry sauce	◎◎	▣▣▣
123	casseroled pheasant	◎◎◎	▣▣
124	oranges in chocolate *or*	◎◎◎	▣▣
	naranjas al kirsch	◎	▣
125	**Winter menu 2**		
127	mushrooms in garlic butter *or*	◎◎◎	▣▣
	orange and celery salad	◎◎	▣
165	garlic bread	◎	▣
128	coddled pockets	◎◎◎	▣▣▣
129	parfait au marron *or*	◎◎◎	▣▣
	flummery Drambuie	◎◎	▣▣
130	**Winter menu 3**		
132	coquilles St Jacques, Hotel de la Poste	◎◎◎	▣▣▣
133	carbonnade flamande	◎	▣▣
134	oeufs à la neige	◎	▣▣▣
135	**Winter menu 4**		
137	iced cucumber soup *or*	◎◎	▣
	celery and almond soup	◎	▣▣
138	ballotine of duck	◎◎◎	▣▣▣
139	toasted savoury cheese *or*	◎	▣
	soft herring roes in white wine	◎◎	▣
140	**Winter menu 5**		
142	avocado mousse aux crevettes *or*	◎◎	▣▣
	Snaffles mousse	◎	▣
143	venison pie	◎◎◎	▣▣▣
144	angel pie	◎◎	▣▣
145	**Winter menu 6**		
147	pickled mushrooms *or*	◎	▣
	avocado au gratin	◎◎	▣

PAGE		COST	EFFORT
148	filets de porc aux pruneaux	◎◎	⊟⊟
149	chocolate whisky gateau	◎◎◎	⊟⊟⊟

150 Winter menu 7

PAGE		COST	EFFORT
152	kipper pâté *or*	◎◎	⊟⊟
	mackerel pâté	◎◎◎	⊟⊟
153	kidneys in Madeira	◎◎	⊟⊟
154	lemon syllabub *or*	◎◎◎	⊟⊟
	quick syllabub	◎◎	⊟

155 Winter menu 8

PAGE		COST	EFFORT
157	terrine de canard aux raisins	◎◎◎	⊟⊟⊟
158	matelote bourgeoise	◎◎◎	⊟⊟⊟
159	ice-cream with butterscotch sauce *or*	◎	⊟
	mint chocolate sauce	◎◎	⊟

Additional recipes

PAGE		COST	EFFORT
160	fresh herring pâté	◎◎	⊟⊟⊟
	Highbullen's guacamole	◎◎	⊟
161	Pink's fish soup	◎◎	⊟⊟
	stuffed aubergine au gratin	◎◎◎	⊟⊟⊟
162	roast duck	◎◎	⊟
163	chicken chanfaina	◎◎	⊟
	moussaka	◎◎	⊟⊟
164	crêpes gruyère	◎◎	⊟⊟⊟
165	hot garlic bread	◎	⊟
	sticky toffee pudding	◎◎	⊟⊟
166	gosebery tarte	◎	⊟
	wholemeal bread	◎	⊟⊟
167	brioche	◎◎	⊟⊟⊟

PAGE	
168	**Basic recipes**
175	**Equivalent temperatures and measures**
175	**Index by restaurant**
178	**General index**
183	**Index of Wines**

Foreword

by Christopher Driver
Editor, *The Good Food Guide*

The Good Food Guide offers its readers critical descriptions of restaurants – of British cooking, that is, in its public aspect. This book is a natural outcrop of the *Guide*. It is designed for sociable lovers of food and wine in their more everyday habitat – the home. But *Guide* restaurants (or rather, restaurants that appeared in the *Guide* in 1971 when this book was first published: there is no '*Guide* restaurant' as such, permanently secure of its place) are the source of the recipes which Mrs Fawcett and Mrs Strang have noted down, tested, and orchestrated here. The echo of folk-song collecting is intentional. Cecil Sharp himself, coaxing a Suffolk wattle-weaver to croak the half-forgotten tunes of his trade, had no harder task than they did, persuading French, Spanish, Chinese, and for that matter British restaurant chefs to identify and quantify the methods and ingredients of their favourite dishes. Occasionally, it must be said, our experiments with a given recipe showed that something essential – a pinch of this or a pound of that, or perhaps only the correct climate and a suitable attitude of mind – had been left out, probably by accident. Professionals often cook, as it were, from a score that provides merely the melody and a figured bass, which their left hands fill in from knowledge and experience. Amateurs, perhaps lacking either the time or the perseverance to perfect a dish before they cook it for company, need to have the harmony written out in full.

This does not imply that the dividing line between professionals and amateurs in cooking runs neatly between the restaurant and the home. Seldom has it ever been as clear-cut as that. The most intricate style of restaurant cuisine must ultimately depend on customers' ability to recognise, not just the refinements, but the rustic or domestic original that has been refined upon. The grandest dish begins with techniques that were probably invented in a cave. The most inventive restaurateurs – Marcel Boulestin springs to mind – learnt the essentials of their craft not in hotel kitchens but at the bottom of their mothers' mixing bowls. And in Britain, especially, public catering itself has given a bad name to the very word 'professional'. For centuries past, discerning foreign visitors have noted that there is far better food to be had in British private houses, often quite simple ones, than in taverns and road-houses, and this judgment has lost none of its force now that the meal in question is much more likely to have been prepared by the mistress (or master) of the house than by a resident cook.

It is true that, taking the post-war period as a whole, restaurants in Britain have improved markedly, for reasons that need not be re-stated here. But then, they could hardly have deteriorated, and it is less often observed that over the same quarter-century there has been a parallel improvement in the food and drink encountered (and expected) at domestic dinner parties. For the first time since the eighteenth century, the art and craft of cooking seem to the British a natural topic of conversation among civilized people. The cross-fertilisation that has taken place between home and restaurant is symbolised by the proprietor of a much-admired restaurant who said with uncommon honesty, on being asked · for a recipe that might appear in this book, that he cooked most of the time from Elizabeth David and did not wish to be accused of plagiarism. (Perhaps cookery writers so influential need an equivalent of the Performing Rights Society, to collect royalties for public presentations of their dishes).

The pages that follow are a further attempt at the same kind of cross-fertili- sation. Not many women feel as easy in a restaurant as they do in their own kitchens, even if they are in male company. This is perhaps because they sense themselves in the presence of a rival. There is something essentially feminine about a good restaurant: it is womb-like, submissive, flattering, and capricious. No wonder men sometimes fall for places which their wives – if they were ever taken along – would see through before the first mouthful. This is why some of *The Good Food Guide*'s most valued correspondents are women, who often notice more, taste more, and possess more technical knowledge than their escorts do. (Would that they also reported twice as often on their dining-out experiences.)

However, though the woman who cooks and entertains skilfully at home has something to teach most restaurants in Britain, the best restaurants also have much to teach amateur cooks. For instance, there are one or two restaurants in the *Guide* which are table d'hôte in the sense that most dinner-parties are table d'hôte: that is, there is no choice on the menu, and once you have sat down you are at the host's mercy. A restaurant so confident in its menu-building will know more than most housewives do about how to please through a studied balance of attractions, and the present writers have carried this idea further in their own presentation of the recipes they have gathered.

In the matter of wine, too, homes and restaurants have been moving closer to each other. The number of restaurants and hotels in Britain that have truly great wine cellars, assembled over decades and lovingly tended by professionals, can almost be counted on the fingers. Most restaurants lack either the capital or the storage space for this kind of thing, and are content, even when their food itself is excellent, to supply the wine-drinker with what is often little more than diabolically expensive plonk. At the same time, there are more and more private houses whose wines, though few and economically bought, are as good as can be found in comparable homes anywhere in the world. Often they have been presciently laid down at opening prices from the lists of serious independent merchants, or picked up later from bin-ends put up for auction.

That may sound like a lot of trouble, but it is the kind of trouble that users of a book like this may well think worth taking, to provide themselves with something a little different for an occasion.

This is, then, a demanding book as well as a seductive one. Its readers and users will, I hope, become demanding diners-out as well as cooks-in, praising the fresh, the seasonal, and the conscientiously-cooked where these things can be found, and where they cannot, politely asking the reason why. For silence is the enemy of good cooking, and for every practitioner who has shot himself on receipt of criticism, there must be twenty who have withered into mediocrity for the want of it. *Bon appétit.*

Introduction

This book has two purposes: to share with a wider public some recipes from restaurants in *The Good Food Guide;* and to incorporate these recipes in balanced menus for dinner parties and other social occasions.

Once we started, it became clear that these aims were at least partly in conflict. Not unnaturally, many restaurants wished to be represented by their most exotic dishes rather than the humble little trick they have with carrots, and most of the recipes we asked for and received seemed to have a higher calorie-count than the average slender woman's daily intake.

Thus it became almost impossible to give truly balanced menus. The meals you will find suggested here are balanced in many other ways, although they tend to be richer than dieticians would like. But this reflects the dining-out habits of the British public. At home people may settle for a light, informal evening meal, but when they eat in a restaurant they are usually ready to tackle three or more substantial courses. Several restaurateurs expressed delight when they heard we were planning this book because, they said, they find it hard to steer people towards any kind of balanced meal. They are often told that their cooking is too rich by a customer who has himself chosen two dishes containing cream, two with pâté, and so on. Not that all restaurateurs are blameless. It is often impossible to avoid having consecutive courses with rich sauces. One thinks wistfully of the perfectly-composed menus at various prices one often meets in France with even the *menu gastronomique* providing an elegant balance.

We have tried to ensure that no dinner party based on this book will totally exhaust the cook or use up a month's housekeeping money. Some meals are obviously more expensive than others. People entertain for many different reasons and besides, one person's special celebrations will be for someone else part of a more routine pattern of entertaining. All the meals take advantage of produce at its seasonal peak, when it is cheaper and tastes better than during the rest of the year.

The calorie-count is not the only factor that affects a meal's balance. You should find in these menus a contrast in flavours, textures and colours, within a course as well as within the menu as a whole. The classic monotonous school meal of steamed cod, cauliflower in white sauce, mashed potatoes and boiled semolina has counterparts on more exalted tables. It is just as aesthetically and dietetically unsuitable to have three courses all containing cream, or several dishes all made in the liquidiser or – unless for deliberate effect – a lurid clash of colours. Good taste is important in menu-planning in its metaphorical as well as its literal sense.

Although the descriptive introduction to each menu may seem dictatorial ('peel the potatoes'; 'drink your sherry'; 'baste the duck'), it represents suggestions only. *Good taste*, like other aesthetic judgments, is in the mind, eye and palate of the beholder, and the reader who wishes to innovate will find that it quickly becomes a habit to assess the qualities of a particular dish so that an appropriate substitute can be produced. We have provided alternative first and third courses, and suggested many others, so that even if you choose to follow the menu plans in the book you will still have considerable variety.

Entertaining

Why are you giving a dinner party anyway? Whatever the real reason – to brighten a dull week, to repay hospitality, to impress the managing director – your guests are probably optimistic enough to assume that you want their company and want them to enjoy themselves. If you cannot convince them of this, send them flowers or a hamper from Fortnum's instead of asking them to dinner. A dinner party is no time to start educating people – at least openly – in eating habits. One restaurateur, according to *The Good Food Guide*, shouted at a woman customer when he saw her putting pepper on his petits pois – tinned, in July. This kind of arrogance has even less place in a private home than in a restaurant, where at least you can have a cathartic row and stalk out. The degree of saltiness you find acceptable is a matter of habit or physiology and it would be pointless to spoil someone's enjoyment of the food you have spent so much time and money on by refusing to have salt and pepper on the table. On the other hand, tolerance has to end somewhere and only a saint will furnish tomato ketchup.

It is not always the hostess's fault when a guest lies awake regretting a second helping of pudding, or even the first. But the hostess has a duty to help by serving food which should not cause her guests discomfort if taken in moderation. She should also offer helpings which are not daunting in size. And most important of all, she must believe guests when they say that they do not want a second helping, or any at all of one particular course. It used to be thought hospitable to force food on people, and polite to refuse the first three offers. We can surely assume that this has passed with a lot of other unnecessary etiquette and believe what we are told the first time.

If you are serving something which is rather unusual or not universally liked, mention it when issuing the dinner invitation. It is easier to say, 'I'm thinking of trying that liver casserole we discovered in Rheims. Do you and John like liver?' than to watch John cutting it up and trying to hide it under the garnish because he has hated liver since childhood.

If you know that friends are slimming, try to provide lots of protein and few calories, so that they need not starve for days as penance for enjoying your party. In our summer menus, for example, fasulya and tortilla mimosa are ideal diet food, and a fresh peach or pear could be offered as an alternative to Mrs. Langan's indecently delectable chocolate pudding.

Shopping

Our cooks were surprised to find that the shopping sometimes took longer than the cooking. Shopping is not generally thought of as a skill, yet even in London, where most things can be found eventually, it requires knowledge and persistence. People in smaller towns or the country are probably all too well aware that they must buy exotic ingredients by post or on expeditions to major shopping centres. It is always worth asking a likely restaurant where they buy a particularly elusive item. It seems almost too obvious to mention that the longer ahead you plan a party, the easier it is to look for rare ingredients. When you have found the best source, or the best brand, of something you often use in your party cooking, it is worth making a note.

Let your regular shopkeepers know that you respect and rely on their skills. An artist choosing brushes or a mother buying shoes for her child expects to spend enough time on the transaction to be satisfied with the purchase. Yet someone buying several pounds' worth of wine or meat often appears almost apologetic to be taking any of the shopkeeper's time.

There *are* still proud specialists in many trades and they should be encouraged by our interest and gratitude rather than allowed to sell out or die off through boredom and neglect. If meat is disappointing, mention it to your butcher – quietly, when the shop is not crowded – and ask how you can ensure that it does not happen again. If you want an elaborate butchering job done, order the meat a day ahead so that he can work on it at leisure rather than in the face of an impatient crowd. When you need fresh herbs, ask in your local shop first. The owner will never know there is a demand for something if you automatically go elsewhere because you are sure it is not obtainable locally.

If you are experimenting with wines, tell the merchant what you are doing and let him know next time you are in how you liked them. You will then be able to judge whether he has enough knowledge and interest to be helpful, or whether you will have to depend on books, newspaper articles and your own experience when making your choice.

Materials

Home-made stock tastes better than water with a bouillon cube dissolved in it, though the latter is quicker and cheaper.

Home-made breadcrumbs look and taste better than orange ones from a packet.

Home-made mayonnaise is completely different from the bottled or even the tubed variety and tastes as good as the oil you use in it.

Olive oil varies greatly in quality and flavour. The most prized is probably a first pressing from Provence; but experiment also with Spanish, Italian and Greek.

Freshly-grated Parmesan cheese tastes totally unlike the pre-packed version which generally contains additional ingredients to stop it caking, and is much dearer.

Garlic is not the same as garlic salt.

Sea-salt and freshly-ground peppercorns have more flavour than their ready-to-use counterparts. Most recipes specified them, but we have mentioned them only where they would greatly affect the flavour or appearance of a dish.

Butter varies greatly in flavour. When a recipe calls for 'good' butter, it does not mean the cheapest 'dairy' butter on sale in England. Normandy butter is perhaps the most suitable.

Fresh tomatoes taste and look quite different from tinned. Some people prefer the tinned ones for soups and sauces.

Fresh herbs are vastly superior to dried and are much less difficult to grow in pots and window-boxes than you might imagine from their scarcity. Dried herbs quickly go stale and lose their flavour, often while acquiring an alien one.

Wine or cider vinegars are gentler than malt and more suitable in most recipes than the fierce brew used to immobilize cockles and chips.

Mustards vary greatly in strength and flavour. Try some of the delicate French ones if you know only strong English ones.

And so we could go on, riding our various hobby-horses. You will surely have many of your own to add.

You can certainly substitute a cube for stock and margarine for olive oil, and leave out the garlic altogether, but you must not then expect your spaghetti sauce to taste like the one you enjoyed so much last summer in Florence. We all use shortcuts and substitutes when they are unavoidable, but if you take pleasure in cooking as an art, you will certainly be aware of the difference compromise makes to the end product.

The liquidiser

Many of the recipes in this book suggest using a liquidiser. In several, a food-mill or a sieve would not produce the same results though in some soups, for example, the slightly rougher texture produced by a food-mill is preferable to the smooth puree that results from liquidising.

The liquidiser has become, in effect, a chef's substitute for the brigade of assistants who used to prepare his sauces and soups and vegetables. Very few restaurants have this kind of staff nowadays; and the go-it-alone school is flourishing, with husband or wife doing most of the cooking and the other partner acting as receptionist, head-waiter, wine-waiter and probably dish-washer too. This is much more like the situation of a hostess giving a dinner party, and a liquidiser will certainly help with some of the more tedious kitchen jobs. For example, as well as making purees, it will grate cheese, grind nuts and make breadcrumbs. Many of us get an aesthetic of sensual pleasure from making mayonnaise, but there must be few who achieve the same glow of satisfaction from pushing a mass of vegetables through a sieve.

The recipes

We have tried to give all the recipes in quantities sufficient for four people, since the arithmetic entailed by increasing the numbers to six or eight is relatively simple. With some soups and sweets, it would be impractical to deal in such small quantities, and in those cases we have indicated the number of helpings. All the recipes given to us by chefs and restaurateurs have been tested in the smaller quantities, and translated into a uniform style. Each restaurateur has approved the edited version of his original recipe. Some of the basic recipes which chefs take for granted – for stocks and sauces and pastry – can be found on page 168.

Liquid measurements are given in fluid ounces. Cups and glasses vary so much that a dish could be unrecognisable as cooked by two different people. All spoonsful mean *level* spoons.

The ingredients are listed in the order of use, and where a recipe involves several different stages (for example, making a tart with a pastry case, filling and topping) the ingredients are grouped together for each stage.

If the chef specified a particular brand, we have given this where the taste is so distinctive that the character of the dish would be altered by using another brand. We have not specified *freshly ground black* pepper in each recipe, although almost every chef asked for it. Flour means plain flour.

The views expressed under *Materials* on page 13 will be a guide to choosing ingredients. We did not use any shortcuts when testing, so that we can vouch for the recipes only using real stock, real mayonnaise, and so on.

The wine notes

We are wine lovers rather than wine experts, and so the suggestions for appropriate wines are offered very tentatively. Even our expert advisers agree that personal taste must play a large part in the selection. Some generalisations are possible – most people find Barsac too sweet for steak but delightful with a fruity pudding; most dislike the odd metallic taste that comes from trying to drink red wine with fish – but beyond that it is a case of experimenting and training your palate. This can be fun as well as instructive, and like-minded friends would probably enjoy an evening or two spent trying out various wines. You are likely to learn more if you choose a theme for such a tasting: clarets of different years; wines made from the same grape in different countries, and so on.

For a tasting or a dinner party, it is worth remembering several basic points:

Plain, clear, stemmed, large-bowled glasses, filled little more than half full, will allow you to appreciate the colour and bouquet of a wine as well as its taste. The stem allows the drinker to keep his hand away from chilled white wines, and makes it easier for him to warm with his hands red wines served rather too cool.

Red wines should be served at room rather than cellar temperature. Even a cheap red wine improves by being decanted and left unstoppered for at least an hour before dinner. An unlabelled wine provokes conversation and amuses or challenges any wine enthusiasts you may have among your guests. Unless you have a cold cellar, you should chill white wines in the refrigerator before serving: a minimum of about 40 minutes for a dry one and up to 90 minutes for a sweet dessert wine. White wines need not be decanted. Dry sherries and aperitifs also benefit from chilling. If you have a good cognac but no balloon glasses, serve it in wine glasses rather than liqueur glasses.

People's capacity for alcohol varies as much as their capacity for food. If people are used to drinking wine with meals they can probably drink at least half a bottle each (more if the aperitif and after-dinner drink are counted in), whereas those who seldom drink table wines may be content with one glass. For a party of four, you will certainly need at least a bottle (six standard glasses) of whatever wine you are serving with the main course. We have frequently suggested a dry sherry or white wine as an aperitif which can be continued through the first course. This is obviously not necessary with soup, but it adds interest to a pâté or fishy first course. Sherry, while it will not keep indefinitely once opened, will taste very good for a week, although the finest finos fade more quickly. If you have decided on a dessert wine, a half-bottle will give four small glasses. Left-over Sauternes will keep for a couple of days in the refrigerator.

The timetables

We have tried to give the average times for each task in preparing one of these meals, but there is no average cook, and you may well find that your private schedule varies greatly from ours. Apart from various skills and awkwardnesses you may have to take into account, you have also been left to put the children to bed and get dressed without our supervision.

It was difficult to decide between preparing all the food beforehand and keeping it warm so that the guests can be given undivided attention, and doing everything as late as possible so that each dish is absolutely fresh. We have compromised, and though most of the preparation is meant to be finished half an hour before dinner, there are jobs to be done in that half hour. Neither the guests nor the food should be sacrificed totally, and no one nowadays expects an unseen staff to be working in the background, so that your short absences should not seem discourteous. Obviously the formality of the party should also be taken into consideration. Nothing is more pleasant than talking to friends in the kitchen while you put the finishing touches to dinner, if all the omens are good. But that could ruin a formal party designed for elegance rather than intimacy.

Cost and effort

On the *Contents* page there are symbols to act as a rough guide to the cost and effort of preparing each dish. This may make it easier to compose different menus based on the recipes in the book.

Acknowledgements

The editors wish to thank all the people, many of them necessarily anonymous, who contributed ideas and criticism to this book. They are particularly grateful for the willing co-operation of busy restaurateurs and for the infinite pains taken by the *Guide's* own staff.

Spring menu 1

almond and watercress soup *or* **tuna and corn bisque**

chicken de Vaux, sauté potatoes, salad

Sailors' Lament (6) *or* **chocolate brandy cake (6–8)**

This meal is very suitable for a family party and for a wide variety of tastes, including children's. All the dishes look well and their ingredients are both familiar and identifiable. Most of them are also inexpensive, so that it will not cost too much to increase quantities for a large party.

The chilled almond and watercress soup would suit a warm spring day and a taste for subtle combinations of flavour. Serve the tuna and corn bisque when it is cooler or when the company is less adventurous. Cream of cauliflower soup (page 112) or spinach soup (page 93) would be other possible choices (with fruit juice ready for any anti-spinach-eaters).

The chicken breasts are easy to serve and eat. They look springlike with their asparagus and tomato garnish. (Frozen asparagus would look just as pretty as fresh; it does not taste the same.) A green salad would be best here: lettuce, watercress, cucumber, green pepper with a mild vinaigrette (page 172).

Both sweets are chocolatey, both mildly alcoholic. If your children (or you on their behalf) dislike the idea of dabbling in spirits at an early age, the chocolate brandy cake might taste rather pleasant without them, but Sailors' Lament, a

custard-filled pie with chocolate topping, would be an insult to the Navy without its tot. The index lists several other chocolate sweets, some of them fit for the nursery.

The almond and watercress soup and the chocolate brandy cake could be made a day ahead. Tuna and corn bisque and Sailors' Lament are better made on the day of the party. The chicken breasts can also be stuffed and the potatoes boiled before the main cooking starts. You will then need about quarter of an hour in the kitchen just before the meal.

If you are feeding children who are known to dislike mushrooms, or who are unenthusiastic about any food not in the tinned junior dinner range, fry one or two chicken breasts without the duxelles stuffing. The odds are that they will demand the stuffed ones and that you will eat the plain, but at least you will have done your duty.

Wine suggestions

MAIN COURSE

EITHER
Alsace Riesling

OR
Portuguese or Loire rosé

The Riesling, a white wine, is fruitier and more expensive than the rosés. The Loire rosé is often drier than Portuguese; the Portuguese is probably easiest of all to obtain. Chill them for an hour.

Timetable

THE DAY BEFORE

Almond and watercress soup – prepare and chill.
Chocolate brandy cake – prepare and chill.

ON THE DAY
morning

Make tuna and corn bisque.
Make Sailors' Lament and chill.

$1\frac{1}{4}$ hours before dinner

Sauté potatoes – boil potatoes until barely tender.
Chicken de Vaux – stuff chicken breasts.
Prepare salad.

$\frac{1}{4}$ hour before

Heat tuna and corn bisque.
Chicken de Vaux – fry chicken and keep warm.
Sauté potatoes. Grill tomatoes and cook asparagus.
Almond and watercress soup – adjust seasoning.
Garnish.

between courses

Toss the salad.

Almond and watercress soup

Le Carrosse, London
chef: Giovanni Borzoni

1 bunch watercress
1 stick of celery
½ pint milk
½ pint single cream
rind of a lemon
1 oz butter
1 oz flour
¾ pint chicken stock (page 171)
3 tablesp ground almonds
salt, pepper

Clean the watercress and save a quarter of it for garnishing. Chop the rest very finely, also the celery. Put them in a saucepan with the milk, cream and the carefully peeled zest of a lemon and bring to the boil.

In a larger saucepan, melt the butter, stir in the flour and cook them together for a few minutes without letting the flour brown. Blend in the chicken stock, a little at a time, to make a thick smooth sauce. Stir into this the milk and cream mixture, then the almonds and some seasoning. Cook gently over a low flame for 10 minutes.

Take out the lemon rind, leave the soup to cool a little and put it in the refrigerator to chill. When it is cold, check the seasoning again and garnish it with the remaining watercress.

Tuna and corn bisque

The Garden, London
chef: Enzo di Battista

3½ oz tin of tuna fish
7 oz tin of corn kernels
2 oz butter
2 oz flour
1 teasp curry powder
½ pint milk
½ pint chicken stock (page 171)
2 tablesp chopped parsley
salt, pepper

Drain the tuna fish and break it into flakes. Drain the corn kernels. Melt the butter in a medium-sized saucepan, stir in the flour and curry powder and let it cook gently for five minutes without browning. Gradually blend in the milk, then the chicken stock and bring to the boil, stirring continuously. Add the tuna, the corn and the parsley and reheat gently. If the soup is too thick, dilute with a little more milk or chicken stock. Season with salt and freshly ground pepper – if the stock is already seasoned, taste before adding more. Serve very hot.

Chicken de Vaux

Open Arms Hotel, Dirleton. H. Johnstone, the chef, named this dish after the first owners of Dirleton Castle.

for the duxelles:
1 small onion
1 oz butter
¼ lb mushrooms
salt, pepper

for the chicken:
4 boned breasts of chicken with wing attached
4 tablesp flour
salt, pepper
1 egg
¼ lb dried breadcrumbs
2 oz butter

for garnishing:
4 medium-sized tomatoes
8 asparagus tips
watercress or parsley

Make the duxelles (page 168).

Remove the skin from the breasts of chicken. Place each piece on a board with the wing uppermost. Cover the breast with a sheet of polythene or waxed paper and gently beat it flat with a meat bat or rolling pin. With the point of a knife, separate the fillet of the breast from the rest of the meat – revealing the cavity between the two. Divide the duxelles among the four pieces of chicken and fill each cavity. Close them up and dust the chicken breasts with seasoned flour. Brush them with beaten egg and coat with breadcrumbs. Heat 2 ounces of butter in a frying-pan and fry the chicken gently for about 4 minutes on each side.

While these are cooking, grill the tomatoes. Cut them in half, season the cut side with salt and pepper, dot with butter and place under a hot grill.

If fresh or frozen asparagus is being used, simmer the tips in salted water for 5 to 10 minutes, then toss in butter. Tinned asparagus tips need only be heated.

To serve, arrange the breasts of chicken down the centre of a heated oval serving dish. Decorate each wing with a cutlet frill and put two asparagus spears on top of each breast. Surround them with the tomatoes and sprigs of watercress or parsley.

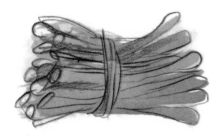

Sailors' Lament (6)

Pengethley Hotel, Ross-on-Wye
chefs: Mrs Harvey and Fraser Carruth.
So named because the first day the Harveys put it on the menu the Navy's rum ration was cancelled.

a cooked flan case
  (6 oz shortcrust pastry – page 173)
2 eggs
2 oz caster sugar
1 teasp cornflour
½ pint milk
1 tablesp gelatine
1 tablesp cold water
2 tablesp dark rum
2 oz plain chocolate
1 fl oz coffee
6 oz double cream

The flan case should be at least 7 inches in diameter, and fairly deep.

Beat the egg yolks with the sugar until they are pale and creamy. Slake the cornflour with a dessertspoonful of the milk and add it to the yolks. Heat the rest of the milk, add it to the egg mixture and cook the custard in a double saucepan until thickened. Dissolve the gelatine in the cold water and add it to the custard. Allow it to cool. Beat the egg whites till stiff and fold them into the custard along with the rum. Fill the flan case and leave it until the mixture has set.

Melt the chocolate in the coffee over hot water. Fold this into the lightly whipped cream. Cover the flan with it and chill until serving time.

Chocolate brandy cake (6-8)

Crispins, London
chef/proprietor: Bruce Copp

¼ lb digestive biscuits
½ lb good dessert chocolate
  e.g. Chocolat-Menier
½ lb butter
2 eggs
3 oz caster sugar
2 oz glacé cherries
2 oz walnut halves
small glass of brandy (or rum)

Crush the digestive biscuits coarsely, and set them aside. Melt the chocolate with the butter over a very low heat. Beat the eggs and sugar together until they are creamy, then beat in the melted chocolate and butter. Fold in three-quarters of the glacé cherries and walnuts, chopped, a small glass of brandy and the crushed biscuits. Put in a suitable buttered mould (or small cake tin). Decorate with the rest of the cherries and walnuts. Store in the refrigerator until about half an hour before serving. Serve in small slices as it is very rich.

Spring menu 2

asparagus flan (4–6) *or* **onion cream tart (4–6)**

stuffed shoulder of veal, paysanne, new potatoes

kishmish *or* **mousse au chocolat (6)**

This menu would make a pleasant Sunday lunch with a roast done in the French fashion. The dishes are colourful, and although they take quite a lot of preparation, none of it is ostentatious and very little of it last-minute. Fellow cooks might make particularly appreciative guests.

The asparagus flan is somewhat lighter than a quiche; the recipe for onion cream tart caps an Alsatian speciality with the olive-and-anchovy garnish of the Provençal pissaladière. The asparagus flan would be quicker to make, the onion cream tart a little more original. If you prefer not to serve pastry at all, you could substitute oeufs Belle Anna (page 45) or guacamole (page 160).

Your butcher will bone the half shoulder of veal more efficiently than you – let him. The veal is nicely brown outside and, because of the fatty pork in the stuffing, it should not dry out during cooking. Carve it in thick slices; the stuffing makes it hard to cut thin ones neatly. Paysanne is a gay mixture of simple vegetables, treated in an interesting way, and all that is needed to complete this course are a few new potatoes, boiled in their skins and tossed in butter.

Some people think that any sweet is all right so long as it is chocolate; for them, obviously, the mousse. Kishmish – a variety of dried fruits cooked with spices and brandy and highly sweetened – makes a change from English and French desserts, though it may be too sweet for some. (You might wish to experiment with different amounts of sugar.) Fresh fruit or cheese could be served instead of either of these sweets.

Although a fair amount of preparation is required, most of it can be done some time beforehand. Both sweets can be made the day before. The pastry and the ingredients for the flans can be prepared well ahead of time so that they can be quickly married up just before they go into the oven. The veal will be roasting before your guests arrive, and the vegetables require very little attention.

Wine suggestions

FIRST COURSE

EITHER	OR
Pouilly-Fumé	Bourgogne Aligoté

Either the Loire wine or the burgundy would go
go well with the creamy first course. Alexis Lichine
can taste cheese and truffles in the
Pouilly-Fumé – can you? Serve chilled.

MAIN COURSE

EITHER	OR
claret (from a single vineyard)	Bourgueil or Valpolicella

The main course needs a lightish red wine. The
second group are cheaper and lighter, but the best
claret you can afford will not be too good.

Timetable

TWO DAYS BEFORE — Kishmish – soak dried fruit.

THE DAY BEFORE — Make kishmish.
or Make mousse au chocolat and chill overnight.

ON THE DAY
morning — Asparagus flan – make pastry; cook asparagus; make
custard.
Onion tart – make pastry.
Stuff shoulder of veal.

$1\frac{3}{4}$ hours before dinner — Pre-heat oven to 400°F, mark 6.
Onion tart – cook onions.
Onion tart or asparagus flan – line flan case.

$1\frac{1}{4}$ hours before — Put veal in the oven to roast.
Prepare paysanne.

$\frac{3}{4}$ hour before — Flan or tart – make up filling.

$\frac{1}{2}$ hour before — Flan or tart – put in oven below meat.
Start cooking paysanne.

$\frac{1}{4}$ hour before — Cook potatoes.

Asparagus flan (4-6)

Peacock Vane, Bonchurch
chef: Joan Wolfenden

6 oz shortcrust pastry (page 173)
½ lb fresh or frozen asparagus
salt
about ¼ pint milk
2 teasp flour
2 large eggs
pepper

Line a buttered 8-inch flan case with the shortcrust pastry. Prick the bottom lightly with a fork.

Trim the asparagus, cut it into 1-inch pieces and cook it in about ¼ pint of salted water. Drain the asparagus; save the water and make it up to ½ pint with milk. Blend the liquid into the flour. Beat the eggs well and add to the milk. Season with plenty of pepper; add more salt if needed.

Put the asparagus in the pastry case. Cover with the custard mixture, and bake in the middle of a fairly hot oven (400°F, mark 6) for 30 minutes.

The flan case, the asparagus and the custard may be prepared some time before, but they should not be married until just before baking; otherwise the flan will be soggy.

Onion cream tart (4-6)

Poacher's Inn, Piddletrenthide
Mrs Fish has adapted this recipe from various sources. It is similar to both the pissaladière found in and around Nice and the Alsatian zewelwaï.

6 oz rich shortcrust pastry
    (page 173)
1½ lb onions
1 oz butter
2 tablesp oil
1 clove garlic
1 egg plus 1 egg yolk
4 tablesp double cream
salt, pepper
12 anchovy fillets
12 stoned green olives

Make the shortcrust pastry and leave it to rest. Slice the onions finely and put them into the heated butter and oil in a saucepan. Cook them very slowly with the lid on until they are soft and golden. Add the crushed garlic half-way through the cooking which may take up to an hour.

Line a buttered 7-inch flan case with the pastry and prick the bottom with a fork. Remove the onions from the heat and add the eggs, beaten with the cream and seasoning. Mix well together, then pour into the flan case. Arrange the anchovies in a criss-cross pattern on top and fill in with the olives.

Place on a baking sheet and cook in the centre of a fairly hot oven (400°F, mark 6) for 30 minutes.

Stuffed shoulder of veal

Mon Plaisir, London
proprietor: Mme Viala chef: Bernard Allaume

a boned half shoulder of veal
  (about 2 lb)
6 oz lean pork
6 oz fatty pork, such as belly
6 oz lean veal
1 small onion
1 clove garlic
¾ oz breadcrumbs
2 tablesp chopped parsley
salt, pepper
fresh or dried sage
fat or dripping

Trim off any excess fat and cut the meat so that it lies in one flat piece.

To make the forcemeat, put the pork and the 6 ounces of veal through the mincer. Chop the onion and garlic. Soak the breadcrumbs in a little milk. Add these to the meat, also the chopped parsley, salt and pepper and a little sage. Mix thoroughly together. Put this stuffing on the veal, roll it up and tie it securely at ½-inch intervals along the roll. Tie a string also from end to end to help keep in the stuffing which tends to swell whilst cooking. Sprinkle with a little salt and pepper.

Put in a roasting tin with a very little fat or dripping, and roast in a hot oven (400°F, mark 6) for about 1½ hours. The meat will give off during cooking some fat and juices which brown in the pan. If a little water is added from time to time as the juices evaporate, the liquid can be used to baste the joint. It will also make a thin but delicious veal gravy to serve with the meat, carved in ½-inch slices.

Paysanne

Au Fin Bec, London
chef: Toni Gretone

¾ lb carrots
½ head of celery
1 small onion
4 oz lean streaky bacon
1 oz butter
2 tablesp olive oil
¼ lb tomatoes, fresh or tinned
¼ pint beef stock (page 170)
salt, pepper
chopped parsley

Clean the carrots and celery and peel the onion. Cut them and the bacon into fairly thin strips – about 2 inches in length. Fry the bacon and the onion in the butter and oil for a minute or two before adding the celery and carrots. Mix gently with a wooden spoon and continue the cooking. When the mixture is hot, stir in the chopped tomatoes and the meat stock, and if it is unseasoned, some salt and pepper. Cover and cook gently on a low flame for about 40 minutes until all the vegetables are cooked. Add a little chopped parsley before serving.

Kishmish

Carpenters Arms, Stanton Wick
Lidia Allcock, the chef, tells us that this is an Armenian sweet.

¼ lb dried figs
¼ lb dried apricots
¼ lb dried soft prunes
¼ lb dried apple rings
¼ lb sultanas
1 oz currants
1 lb sugar
1 strip lemon rind
½ dessertsp mixed nutmeg,
cinnamon, allspice and cloves
1 tablesp brandy
cream

Remove the stalks from the figs. Wash all the fruit and put it in a bowl with 1½ pints of water. Leave to soak overnight. Next day, strain off the soaking water into an enamelled saucepan, add the sugar, lemon rind and spices and let them simmer together for 10 minutes. Then add the fruit and continue to cook very gently until all the fruit is tender. This will take up to an hour. Leave to cool.

When the mixture is cold, remove lemon rind and stir in the brandy. Serve with cream and with one of the prunes on top of each helping.

Mousse au chocolat (6)

Brompton Grill, London
chef: K. Kouloumas

½ lb good dessert or bitter
    chocolate
2½ fl oz milk
1 tablesp rum (or an orange
    liqueur)
2½ fl oz double cream
4 egg whites
1 dessertsp caster sugar

Break up or grate the chocolate into a double boiler, or into a pan set over another containing simmering water. While it is melting over a low flame, stir it occasionally. Heat the milk.

When the chocolate has melted, pour into it the hot milk and the rum and mix them together. Leave the mixture to cool. Lightly whip the cream but do not let it get too thick or it will not fold easily into the mousse.

In a separate bowl, whisk the egg whites until they are very stiff and beat in the sugar.

Fold first the whipped cream into the cooled chocolate and then the whipped egg whites, as quickly and lightly as possible.

Spoon the mousse into individual glasses or dishes or into a large serving bowl, and put it into the refrigerator to firm for at least 4 hours, but preferably overnight.

Spring menu 3

spiced spare ribs *or* **spare ribs in honey**

turbot kebabs with shrimp sauce, pilaff, salad

orange caramel trifle (6)

The first and main courses of this meal are rather luxurious, and immediately appealing to eye and palate. You could use this menu for all but the most rigidly meat-and-two-veg guests, and even those who look on fish as a stopgap between the soup and the roast will be tolerant after gnawing on their spare ribs. The crunchy caramel topping makes the sweet a schoolboy's delight but the fresh fruit and liqueur help it to please adults too.

Choose the North Chinese ribs for guests who know and enjoy Chinese cooking. (The star anise is obtainable from Chinese stores and also from some that sell Indian spices.) The honey-baked ribs are sweeter and rather simpler in flavour than the others. In either case, provide finger bowls and napkins to encourage everyone to eat the ribs in their fingers. If you cannot find a butcher who will cut pork in this way (it is worth asking in your local Chinese restaurant where they buy their meat), or if you prefer something less messy to eat, you could substitute Oak House pâté (page 83) or terrine de campagne (page 45).

The turbot kebabs look pretty, with the white fish set off by red tomatoes and the green bay leaves (use young, bright ones if you happen to have your own tree); the tomatoes and peas in the pilaff echo this colour contrast. Since the kebabs slide off the skewers quite easily, allow the guests to do the job them-selves if they are willing. Offer the sauce and a simple green salad separately. If your guests have small appetites or large waistlines, cheese or fresh fruit might be a better idea than the trifle.

Since you will need about twenty minutes in the kitchen just before dinner, this meal would be most suitable for guests whom you know well, so that you may abandon them comfortably during this time. But if the conversation is too interesting to miss completely, it can all be done in a series of five-minute dashes. Unless you have a built-in time clock and docile guests, it would probably be safer to finish cooking the kebabs just before dinner and keep them warm until they are needed.

Wine Suggestions

	APERITIF AND FIRST COURSE	EITHER Manzanilla	OR dry Fino

The rich, sweetish pork would be set off by a really dry chilled sherry.

	MAIN COURSE	EITHER white burgundy (Meursault, Chassagne- Montrachet)	OR hock (say, Johannisberger or Kreuznacher)

A reliable burgundy or good hock will complement the fish. Serve chilled.

	DESSERT	EITHER white Bordeaux (Cérons, Loupiac)	OR Ch. d'Yquem

If the meal celebrates an inheritance, have a dessert wine; if it is a large inheritance, choose the Ch. d'Yquem. Chill well. Cheeselovers would appreciate a glass of claret or burgundy instead, or as well, after so much white wine.

Timetable

	THE DAY BEFORE	Spiced spare ribs – marinate ribs overnight.

ON THE DAY

	morning	Make orange caramel trifle and chill it.
	5½ hours before dinner	Spare ribs in honey – make marinade and soak ribs.
	2¾ hours before	Spare ribs in honey – pre-heat oven to 400°F, mark 6.
	2½ hours before	Spare ribs in honey – put in oven.
	2 hours before	Spiced spare ribs – start cooking.
	1–1½ hours before	Spare ribs in honey – drain and reserve half the honey liquor and reduce oven heat to 350°F, mark 4. Cut up the turbot and marinate it. Prepare shrimp sauce.
	¾ hour before	Turbot – prepare skewers. Pilaff – start preparation.
	¼ hour before	Spare ribs in honey put the ribs in a pan with liquor to reduce. Reduce oven heat to warming temperature. Cook kebabs and keep them warm.
	5 mins. before	Put rice to cook in stock.
	between courses	Complete the pilaff and toss salad.

Spiced spare ribs

Lee Yuan, London
Mr Lee tells us that these ribs are served in the North Chinese style, with no sauce.

2 lb pork spare ribs
¾ pint soy sauce
6 star anise (Chinese)
12 black peppercorns
1 dessertsp brown sugar
2 fl oz dry sherry

The ribs should be cut Chinese-style by your butcher: 3 to 4 inches long and evened at the ends. Cut between the ribs so that they are all separate and marinate them overnight in the soy, anise, crushed peppercorns, sugar and sherry. Turn them occasionally.

Drain the ribs and put them in a pan with enough cold water to come about half-way up – less than a pint should do. Simmer them for 2 hours, uncovered, until all the water has gone. Turn them frequently. They are then cooked and can be served immediately or reheated quickly in a frying-pan with a little oil just before serving.

EDITOR'S NOTE: soy sauce varies considerably in strength and saltiness. If yours is a very tangy one, rinse the ribs when you take then from the marinade, so that the finished dish will not be too salty. The marinade can be saved and used again.

Spare ribs in honey

Bumbles, London
chef: David Prentice

2 lb pork spare ribs
5 tablesp tomato ketchup
2 tablesp clear honey
2 tablesp soy sauce
3 tablesp wine vinegar
½ tablesp tomato puree
½ pint beef stock (page 170)
1 teasp salt

Spread out the ribs, cut as in the previous recipe, in a roasting tin. Mix together all the remaining ingredients and pour over the ribs. Leave in a cool place for 2 or 3 hours, turning the ribs from time to time.

Roast the ribs in the marinade in the oven for 1 hour at 400°F, mark 6; turn them during cooking to prevent scorching the bone. Pour off half the liquor and reserve it. Reduce the oven heat to moderate (350°F, mark 4) and continue roasting, still turning until the meat is cooked and a rich brown – another 1 to 1½ hours. Add the remaining liquor to that already saved.

Fifteen minutes before serving, put the ribs into a frying-pan with about half a pint of the liquor and cook them quickly on a high flame, turning them once or twice, so that the liquor is reduced to a thick syrup and the ribs are hot. Serve them in their sauce.

Turbot kebabs with shrimp sauce

Emlyn Arms Hotel, Newcastle Emlyn
Eric Llewellyn enjoyed this dish so much in the south of France that his wife, Ann, re-invented it for him.

for the marinade:
1½–1¾ lb skinned and filleted turbot
2 tablesp olive oil
juice of ½ lemon
salt, pepper

for the sauce:
1 small onion or shallot
1 oz butter
1 oz flour
¾ pint milk
3 oz shelled shrimps or prawns,
    fresh or frozen
small bay leaf
a little tomato puree
2 or 3 drops Tabasco
1 tablesp cream

for the skewers:
8 small tomatoes
8–12 bay leaves, preferably fresh
pilaff (page 174)

Cut the turbot into 1–1½ inch cubes. Mix together the olive oil, lemon juice, a little salt and pepper and pour this over the fish. Cover it and leave it for half an hour, turning the fish from time to time.

Meanwhile, prepare the shrimp sauce. Chop the onion or shallot finely and cook it in the butter until it is transparent. Stir in the flour and let it cook a little before blending in the milk. Bring it to the boil, stirring constantly, and when it has thickened, add the shrimps, bay leaf and enough tomato puree to colour the sauce pink.

Adjust the seasoning, add the Tabasco, and leave to simmer on a very low heat for 10 minutes. If the sauce is then to stand for any time, cover it with a buttered paper (page 174).

Take 8 skewers about 9 inches long and thread on to them, one after the other, a piece of turbot, a quarter of tomato, a piece of bay leaf, a piece of turbot and so on. Each skewer should take about 5 pieces of fish, 4 quarters of tomato and 1 or 2 bay leaves. Arrange the skewers on the rack of the grill pan, pour half the marinade over them and put under a hot grill for 5–7 minutes each side, basting them with the marinade after turning them.

While the kebabs are grilling, reheat the sauce and stir a tablespoonful of cream into it. Arrange the kebabs on a bed of pilaff (page 174) and serve the sauce separately.

Orange caramel trifle (6)

Romans, Silchester
Louis Bielski, the chef, first ate this at the Spread Eagle at Thame when he was an Oxford undergraduate in the thirties. It was one of John Fothergill's recipes.

for the caramel
6 oz sugar
3 fl oz water

for the custard
2 egg yolks
½ pint milk
1 dessertsp sugar

for the trifle
8 small trifle sponges
4 oranges plus the juice of 1 orange
1 tablesp orange liqueur (curaçao, Cointreau, Grand Marnier)
½ pint double cream
6 lumps of sugar

First make the caramel so that it has time to cool. Heat the sugar slowly with the water in a small, heavy saucepan. Boil without stirring until it turns barley-sugar colour. As soon as it does so, and before it has time to become too burnt, pour it on to a greased pie dish or tray in a very thin layer, and leave it to set. When the caramel is cold, break it into small, crunchy pieces.

Make a custard by heating the milk and pouring it onto the beaten egg yolks and sugar. Return the mixture to the rinsed pan and heat gently, stirring continuously, until it thickens, but without letting it boil. (Use a double boiler if you have one.) Put aside to get cold.

Line the bottom of a glass dish with the sponges. Peel the oranges, remove all the pith, cut the segments into two or three pieces and lay them on top of the sponge. Mix together the orange juice and the liqueur and pour it over. Follow this with a covering of the custard, then with a layer of orange-flavoured whipped cream, made by rubbing the sugar lumps over the skins of the oranges to absorb the flavour before beating them into the cream. The cream can be piped or spooned over the top, and then the whole sprinkled with the crunchy caramel.

Spring menu 4

pignatelle (pine cones)

braised beef in red wine, cabbage with onion, new potatoes

brown bread ice-cream *or* **caramel ice-cream**

For a cool spring evening, possibly after energetic walking or gardening, this is a comforting meal, neither expensive nor elaborate. It could be dressed up for a formal party but seems more appropriate for close friends, comfortable clothes and a relaxed atmosphere. It is by no means dull, with an original first course and unexpected ice-creams.

The pignatelle are little savoury puffs of choux pastry, flavoured with ham and cheese, which take irregular shapes as they cook. Since they require deep-frying and should be eaten as fresh as possible, you will probably prefer to serve them to be eaten in the fingers with an aperitif rather than at table as a formal first course. If you have the right kind of kitchen, friends and temperament, let them take their sherry into the kitchen while you cook, so that each batch can be eaten the moment it is ready. If all this sounds rather daunting, and if you hate the smells of fat and cabbage, serve a fish pâté instead: smoked trout pâté (page 40) or fresh herring pâté (page 160) with brown bread (page 166) and butter.

The braised beef has a rich sauce reminiscent of boeuf bourguignonne. If you do not want to serve cabbage and potatoes with it, rice and a salad would be just as suitable.

Both the sweets are based on the very simplest ice of all – frozen cream. They taste delicious but lack the stability of a custard ice-cream and therefore should be taken from the freezing compartment only at the very last minute. Caramel ice-cream tastes as you would expect; the brown bread one will pleasantly surprise you if you find the name off-putting, since it tastes almost like a hazelnut praline ice. If you do not have an adequate freezing compartment in your refrigerator, choose naranjas al kirsch (page 124) or angel pie (page 144) instead.

The preparation of all of this meal except the pignatelle is very flexible indeed. The braised beef (which reheats well) and the ice-cream can be made the day before or on the morning of the party. The pignatelle can be mixed while the fat is heating and you can keep an eye on the cabbage while the last batches are being fried.

Wine suggestions

APERITIF AND
FIRST COURSE

EITHER   OR

dry Montilla   dry sherry

Montilla will be harder to find but it is very appropriate to drink through the first course. Serve either chilled.

MAIN COURSE

EITHER   OR

red burgundy   Barolo or Rioja

Since this is a French dish, you might want a French wine – a better version of whatever you used to braise the beef. The Italian and Spanish wines would be equally suitable for both cooking and drinking. They would all be strong enough to compete with the flavours in the main dish.

Timetable

THE DAY BEFORE

Make ice-cream.
Braised beef – prepare meat and marinate overnight.

ON THE DAY

$2\frac{1}{4}$ hours before dinner

Braised beef – fry beef. Prepare and fry other ingredients.

$1\frac{3}{4}$ hours before

Leave beef and other ingredients to simmer slowly in stock.

$\frac{3}{4}$ hours before

Pignatelle – make choux pastry.

$\frac{1}{2}$ hour before

Prepare cabbage.
Pignatelle – heat fat or oil.

20 mins. before

Mix pignatelle.

10–15 mins. before

Fry pignatelle.
Cook cabbage and keep it warm.

Pignatelle

Lowbyer Manor Hotel, Alston
chef/proprietor: Mrs Miller

¼ pint water
1½ oz butter
salt, pepper
2½ oz sifted flour
2 small eggs
1 thick slice lean ham
2 oz strong cheese (e.g.
   Lancashire)
oil for deep frying

To make the choux pastry, bring
the water to the boil with the butter
and some salt and pepper. When the
butter has melted, remove from the
heat and add the flour all at once.
Beat well until the flour is thoroughly
blended, then return to a moderate
heat for a minute or two until the
mixture leaves the sides of the pan
to form a ball. Remove from the heat
and beat the eggs in, one at a time,
beating hard after each addition
(this can be done easily with an
electric mixer). Dice the ham and
grate the cheese and stir them into
the mixture.

Heat some deep fat or oil until it is
very hot (375°F). Drop 5 or 6 teaspoonsful of the pastry mixture into
the fat, and fry them for about two
minutes, by which time they should
have puffed up into odd shapes and
turned golden brown. Keep the heat
fairly high, since the mixture cools
the fat.

Drain the pine cones on absorbent
paper and keep them hot under
the grill or in the oven while cooking
subsequent batches – they should
be served very hot and as soon after
cooking as possible.

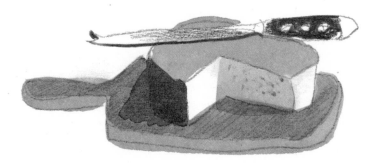

Braised beef in red wine

Mill House Restaurant, Milford-on-Sea
chef/proprietors: Mr & Mrs Colin Cooper-English

1¼ lb topside of beef
¼ bottle red wine, preferably
   burgundy
4–6 tablesp oil
1 pint beef stock (page 170)
2 oz flour
salt, pepper
2–3 oz streaky bacon
2 onions
2 carrots
1 oz tomato puree
1 pinch powdered thyme
1 pinch powdered marjoram
1 bouquet garni (page 168)
1 garlic clove
½ lb button mushrooms
chopped parsley

Trim the meat and cut in ½-inch cubes. Marinate it covered in the refrigerator overnight in the wine and about 2 tablespoonsful of the oil. Heat the stock in a large, heavy saucepan. Drain the beef well and toss it in seasoned flour. Fry it quickly in the hot oil until brown. Add it to the hot stock which must only simmer, since boiling would toughen the meat.

Chop the bacon and fry it until the fat begins to run. Add the sliced onions and carrots and fry them until the onion is slightly softened.

Stir in the tomato puree and cook until it darkens a little. Stir in the herbs and crushed garlic and fry the mixture for one or two minutes. Add the vegetables to the stock along with the residue of the marinade and the whole mushrooms. Simmer gently for 2 hours, skimming occasionally.

Before serving, remove the bouquet garni, adjust the seasoning and consistency (with stock or arrowroot) and garnish with chopped parsley.

Cabbage with onion

Bay Horse Inn, Winton
chef: Sylvia Gilson

1 small hard white cabbage
2 teasp coarse salt
2 oz butter
1 medium-sized onion
black pepper

Shred the cabbage fairly finely, sprinkle it with the salt and soak it for 10 minutes in cold water. Drain off the water but do not wash off the salt. Melt an ounce of the butter in a large saucepan, add the cabbage and cook it until it is tender, shaking the pan frequently to prevent sticking.

Turn out into a colander. In the same pan fry the chopped onion in the rest of the butter. When it is golden, stir in the cabbage and continue to cook for a minute or two. Add plenty of black pepper, stir well and serve.

Brown bread ice-cream

Wife of Bath, Wye
chef/proprietor: Michael Waterfield

½ pint double cream
1 oz vanilla sugar (page 169)
3 oz stale brown bread
3 oz soft, dark brown sugar
brandy

Make the ice-cream by whipping the cream and caster sugar lightly. Turn it into an ice tray or polythene container, cover and put in the freezing compartment of the refrigerator, turned to its lowest number. As the mixture begins to harden round the edges, stir the sides into the middle. Make breadcrumbs from the stale brown bread. Lay these out on an oiled baking tray and sprinkle with brown sugar. Put them in a fairly hot oven (400°F, mark 6) or under the grill until the sugar caramelises with the bread. Stir from time to time. When they are golden brown, leave them to cool and break them up again into crumbs.

When the ice-cream is semi-stiff, mix in the crumbs. Put it back in the freezing compartment and freeze for another 2 hours.

Pour a little brandy over each portion before serving.

Caramel ice-cream

Ballymaloe House, Shanagarry
chef: Mrs M. Allen

4 tablesp granulated sugar
2 egg yolks
½ pint double cream

Put the sugar in a pan with 2 tablespoonsful of water over a moderate heat until the sugar has dissolved completely. Then let the sugar boil, swirling the pan occasionally, until it turns a light brown colour. Pour 4 tablespoonsful of water into the caramel and simmer, stirring, until it has melted.

Beat the egg yolks, pour the syrup into them slowly, continuing to beat until the mixture thickens. Whip the cream and fold it into the mixture. Turn it into a metal or polythene mould, cover and put in the freezing compartment of the refrigerator at its lowest number. It will be frozen after about 2 hours.

EDITOR'S NOTE: broken walnuts would make an attractive garnish.

Spring menu 5

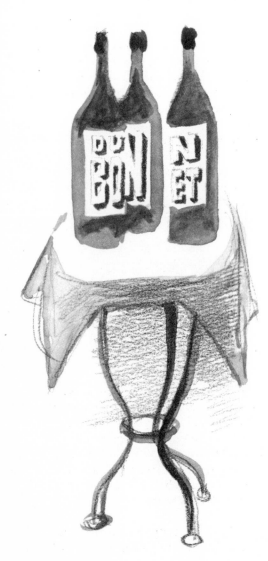

avocado mousse (6) *or* **smoked trout pâté (4–6)**

liver with Dubonnet and orange, rice, salad

gateau Fontes *or* **Lockets savoury**

Invite friends whose tastes you know, since liver is not everyone's meat. The pale delicate mousses contrast with the vivid colours of the orange and parsley in the sauce with the liver, which in turn gives way to the coffee-and-cream of gateau Fontes (or pears and Stilton, if you serve the savoury). This menu attempts to balance costs by combining the relatively expensive first and last courses with a fairly inexpensive main dish. If you wish to economise more rigorously, substitute fresh herring pâté (page 160) or marinated kipper fillets (page 88) for the mousses, and any of the non-fruity puddings for the sweet or savoury: perhaps oeufs à la neige (page 134) or brown bread ice-cream (page 37).

The trout pâté, which is itself mousse-like in consistency, could be made the day before the dinner party. The avocados need only a short chilling time and will discolour if left for too long. Both are so good that you might as well choose the flavour you prefer or the one which your china will set off best. (The avocado mousse is pale green and the trout pâté creamy white.)

The liver with Dubonnet and orange has an interesting tangy sauce with an undertone of sweetness. It should not be overcooked, since liver toughens very quickly. Rice to absorb the sauce and a green salad are all that are needed to complete the course.

Once again, knowledge of your friends' tastes will guide you in your choice of sweet or savoury. Gateau Fontes has a strong, pure coffee flavour, mellowed by the ground almonds and biscuits. It looks dramatic with its whipped cream coating and toasted almond garnish. On the other hand, after the slight sweetness of the sauce with the liver, some people might prefer to serve Lockets savoury (watercress, sliced pears and Stilton on toast, heated in the oven) and keep the wine circulating. If you choose the savoury, you might decide not to serve a salad since there is a good helping of watercress here. Another point to consider is that the gateau can be made a day ahead, while the savoury requires last-minute attention. Petits fours with the coffee would be particularly appropriate after the savoury.

This meal is going to keep you in the kitchen for twenty minutes or so before dinner, cooking the liver and making its sauce. But the mousse, the pâté and the gateau can all be made ahead of time, and only if you choose the savoury need you be a further five minutes away from your guests.

Wine suggestions

APERITIF	EITHER	OR
	Chambéry	Gewürztraminer

Smoked trout calls for a glass of something white: choose Chambéry if you like a dry white vermouth – and if you can find it – or the spicy Gewürztraminer. Chill.

MAIN COURSE	EITHER	OR
	Chinon or Bourgueil	Bulgarian Gamza or Rumanian Cabernet

The sweetish orange sauce makes this a difficult dish for wine. All the above wines are inexpensive. The Touraine ones are lighter, but rather hard to find; the Rumanian wine is very slightly sweet.

Timetable

THE DAY BEFORE	Make gateau Fontes and chill it overnight.
ON THE DAY	
morning	Make smoked trout pâté and chill it.
3¾ hours before dinner	Avocado mousse – prepare marinade and avocados and leave to marinate.
2¾ hours before	Avocado mousse – make and chill.
1½ hours before	Liver with Dubonnet – prepare ingredients. Gateau Fontes – complete the preparation. Prepare salad. Avocado mousse – prepare smoked salmon and garnishes.
½ hour before	Pre-heat oven to 350°F, mark 4. Prepare Lockets savoury.
¼ hour before	Cook rice. Cook liver and keep it warm.
5 mins. before	Avocado mousse – complete preparation.
between courses	Toss salad.
after main course	Heat Lockets savoury for 5 minutes in the oven.

Avocado mousse (6)

The Priory, Bath
chef/proprietor: Thea Dupays

2 ripe avocados
6–8 tablesp vinaigrette (page 172)
2 tablesp mayonnaise (page 171)
2 tablesp double cream, lightly
 whipped
1 lemon
salt, pepper
2 oz smoked salmon
¼ lb prawns
cucumber

Remove the stones and skins from the avocados and cut them into slices. Leave to marinate for an hour in the vinaigrette. Then put through a liquidiser with the marinade. If the pears are not completely soft, squash them first with a fork, or add a little more dressing to help to puree them smoothly. Mix in the mayonnaise, whipped cream and the juice of half a lemon. Check the seasoning, and chill, covered, in the refrigerator.

Just before serving, dice the smoked salmon and fold it in. Serve in individual ramekins or glass dishes, decorated with the prawns, sliced cucumber and lemon.

CHEF'S NOTE: avocados which appear to be overripe, but are not actually bad, are perfect for this dish. The smoked salmon can be off-cuts from the tail or the head.

EDITOR'S NOTE: although this dish should be made some hours before serving, it should not be kept overnight, since the avocado will discolour.

Smoked trout pâté (4-6)

Lacy's, London
chef: Bill Lacy

2 smoked trout, about 5 oz each
¼ pint soured cream
5 oz cottage cheese
juice of ½ large lemon
salt, pepper
parsley, lemon slices

Remove the skin and bones from the trout and flake them into the liquidiser. Add the soured cream and then the sieved cottage cheese and blend until smooth. Season to taste with lemon juice, salt and pepper. Pack into cocotte dishes and chill.

Garnish with a sprig of parsley or slice of lemon and serve with hot, brown toast.

EDITOR'S NOTE: if the mixture does not 'turn' easily in your liquidiser, either do the blending in two batches or add a little single cream.

If you are using larger trout, increase the quantities of soured cream and cottage cheese.

Liver with Dubonnet and orange

Lacy's, London
chef: Bill Lacy

1 lb lamb's liver
1 tablesp olive oil
1½ oz butter
2 shallots or small onions
1 clove garlic
seasoned flour
1 tablesp orange juice
4 fl oz red Dubonnet
2 tablesp finely chopped parsley
coarsely grated rind of 1 large
    orange
1 teasp finely grated lemon rind

Either ask the butcher to cut the liver in even slices, just under ½ inch thick, or buy it in the piece and cut it yourself.

Heat the oil and butter in a large frying-pan over a low heat. In it cook the very finely chopped onions and the crushed garlic, covered and still over a low heat, until the onions are soft and beginning to colour. Coat liver slices with seasoned flour and put them in the pan in one layer. Continue to cook over very moderate heat. As soon as the blood rises, turn the liver and cook it for a rather shorter time at an even lower heat. Remove the slices to a warm plate and keep them hot.

Add the orange juice and Dubonnet to the onions and juices left in the pan, scraping the bottom with a wooden spoon or spatula. Bring to the boil and cook rapidly for a few minutes until the sauce has reduced by almost half. Strain it and return it to the pan. Lower the heat, add the parsley, orange rind and lemon rind (keeping some of the orange rind and parsley for a garnish) and stir the sauce until it reaches boiling point. Pour it over the liver and serve at once.

EDITOR'S NOTE: the cooking time will depend on the thickness of the liver and on personal taste, but the liver must not be overcooked.
If your frying-pan has no lid, use aluminium foil.

Gateau Fontes

The Hat and Feather, Knutsford
chef: Mrs Stirling
Mrs Stirling and her friend Mrs Fontes first ate a chocolate version of this gateau in a London restaurant. They enjoyed it so much that they created this variation.

6 fl oz strong, medium sweet Turkish or espresso coffee
¼ lb butter
¼ lb sugar
¼ lb ground almonds
1 egg
¼ lb Marie biscuits
¼–½ pint double cream
1 liqueur glass Tia Maria
1–2 oz slivered almonds

Heat the coffee and in it melt the butter and sugar. Stir in the ground almonds and the egg. Heat slowly, stirring all the time until the mixture has thickened slightly. (Do not boil or the egg will scramble.) Cool slightly. Break the biscuits into small pieces, not crumbs, and fold them into the mixture. Turn it into a buttered, one-pint pudding basin and refrigerate it overnight.

To serve, turn out the pudding onto a flat dish, cover it with the whipped cream into which the liqueur has been beaten and decorate with toasted, slivered almonds. Hedgehog style looks quite striking.

Lockets savoury

Lockets, London
chef: Franz Vojtisek

8 small slices of white bread
1 or 2 bunches of watercress
4 ripe pears
12 oz Stilton cheese
freshly ground black pepper

Toast the slices of bread, trim off the crusts and put them into 4 individual ovenproof dishes. Spread some watercress evenly over each slice.

Peel and core the pears, cut them in thin slices and arrange them on top of the watercress. Slice the Stilton and cover the pears with it.

Put the savouries into a moderate oven (350°F, mark 4) to cook for about 5 minutes until the cheese has melted. Grind a little black pepper on top before serving.

Spring menu 6

terrine de campagne (6) *or* **oeufs Belle Anna**

agnello e patate alla Villa Cesare, broccoli

spiced pears *or* **cheese and fresh fruit**

Choose a special occasion and discriminating guests for this elegant, expensive meal. The rough, country terrine prepares the way for the more delicate – but still garlicky – racks of lamb on their bed of truffled potatoes. The sweet is simple but made interesting by the spices and cider used with the pears.

If you know that your guests enjoy strong, peasanty flavours, serve the terrine as the first course. It keeps well for a few days and seems to mellow somewhat during that time. Otherwise, try oeufs Belle Anna, which are hard-boiled eggs stuffed with the yolks, pâté de foie truffé and mayonnaise, with a shrimp garnish.

It is worth buying the best lamb you can afford. In early spring, English lamb produces delicious cutlets, which it would be a sin to overcook. If any of your guests will not eat lamb pink inside, change the menu – or the guests. The contrast of crisp, golden crumbs flecked with herbs and the delicate pink meat is a major pleasure of the dish. The potatoes will brown only slightly and the lamb should be carved in the kitchen and dressed neatly on top of them. If you have a little tin of truffles, the potatoes will taste even better than with mushrooms, and you should then avoid using a truffled pâté in the first course. Broccoli goes well with the spring lamb and needs only butter to accentuate its flavour and colour.

After all this richness the pears in cider will be a refreshing contrast and a change from the more usual pears in red wine. Cheese and fruit would be the better alternative if you are enjoying a good wine and have enough left to carry you through the dessert.

The terrine and spiced pears can be prepared far enough ahead of the meal for you to give the lamb full attention. As noted in the recipe, ovens vary greatly in their speed of reaction to changes, and you may find that our timing is wrong for your oven. If the guests are the discriminating ones we suggested, they will have patience enough to wait until the lamb is ready – a better approach than the risk of overcooking it. It is not an easy dish to keep hot, since the crumb coating must be crisp and yet not burned. You may feel that a practice run on New Zealand lamb for the family would better equip you to cope with these difficulties.

EITHER	OR
dry white burgundy	dry Hungarian white
(Mâcon Viré)	or Soave

The dry white burgundy would have enough body to stand up to the strong-flavoured terrine. The Hungarian and Italian wines are less dry. None of these wines should cost a great deal; all should be chilled.

MAIN COURSE

EITHER	OR
a good claret	Beaujolais (Fleurie)
(Ch. Palmer,	
Ch. Montrose, Ch. Léo-	
ville-Lascases)	

A first-class claret of sufficient age – not less than 7–8 years – will be smooth, full and balanced. For something lighter, perhaps more springlike, and certainly cheaper, try a 2- to 4-year-old Beaujolais, preferably from a named district.

Timetable

ONE OR TWO DAYS BEFORE · Make terrine de campagne.

ON THE DAY

morning · Prepare spiced pears and chill them.

Oeufs Belle Anna – hard-boil eggs; make mayonnaise.

$1\frac{1}{2}$ hours before dinner · Pre-heat oven to 375°F, mark 5.

Agnello e patate – prepare crumbs and potatoes.

$1\frac{1}{4}$ hours before · Put potatoes in oven for $\frac{1}{2}$ hour.

1 hour before · Make up oeufs Belle Anna.

$\frac{3}{4}$ hour before · Increase oven heat. Roast lamb for 12–15 minutes.

$\frac{1}{2}$ hour before · Increase oven heat again. Roll lamb in breadcrumbs, coat with melted butter and return to oven for 10–15 minutes.

Remove foil to allow patate to brown.

$\frac{1}{4}$ hour before · Prepare lamb for serving and keep it warm.

Just before · Spiced pears – whip the cream.

Terrine – make toast.

Terrine de campagne (6)

Bistro Angeline, Salem
chef: Mrs Jacob

½ lb fatty, left-over cooked pork
  (or ¾ lb belly of pork)
¼ lb veal
½ lb chicken or ox liver
2 small cloves garlic
1 tablesp chopped parsley
2 tablesp brandy
salt, pepper
4 slices unsmoked bacon
bay leaf
sprig of thyme
2 tablesp flour

If you have no left-over pork, cook the belly of pork for 30 minutes at 400°F, mark 6.

Put the pork, veal and liver through the coarsest blade of the mincer. Mix well, then add the chopped garlic, parsley, brandy, salt and pepper and mix again thoroughly. Line a small terrine with the bacon, and pack the mixture firmly into it.

Place the bay leaf and thyme on top.

Make a smooth paste with the flour and a little water and seal the join between the lid and the terrine. Stand the terrine in a bain-marie (page 168) and cook in a moderate oven (350°F, mark 4) for 1–1½ hours.

Let the pâté cool completely before removing the lid.

Oeufs Belle Anna

Clifton Hotel, Nairn
chef/proprietor: Gordon Macintyre
Anna was a beautiful French blonde who worked in Mr Macintyre's kitchen some years ago. She loved cooking – and Rossini – and these eggs were a particular favourite of hers.

4 large eggs
3 oz pâté de foie truffé
2–3 tablesp mayonnaise (page 171)
heart of a lettuce
2 oz shelled shrimps, fresh or
  frozen

Hard boil the eggs. When they have cooled, shell them and cut them in half lengthways. Take out the yolks and rub them through a fine sieve.

Mash the pâté with a fork and mix it with the egg. Stir in enough mayonnaise to bind the pâté and egg

but not enough to mask the flavour of the pâté.

Pile the mixture back into the whites of the eggs and arrange these on a bed of lettuce leaves, sprinkling their tops with the pink shrimps.

Agnello e patate alla Villa Cesare

Tiberio, London
executive chef: Carlo Avogadri

**2 racks of lamb (best end of neck),
  each with 6 cutlets**
¼ lb fresh white breadcrumbs
1 tablesp chopped parsley
2 cloves garlic
2 sprigs thyme
salt, pepper
2 lb potatoes (peeled weight)
1 truffle or 8 button mushrooms
3–4 oz butter
**½ pint veal or chicken stock
  (page 171)**
1 oz Parmesan cheese
watercress

Ask the butcher to skin and chine the lamb and cut the bones off an inch above the nut of flesh. Mix the breadcrumbs, parsley, chopped garlic, chopped thyme and salt and pepper.

Butter the surface of a large gratin or other fireproof dish. Slice the potatoes finely and layer them neatly with the chopped truffle or mushrooms and the grated cheese. The dish should be covered to the depth of one inch. Add about 1½ ounces of butter in small pieces, and salt and pepper. Pour over the stock and cover the dish with greaseproof paper or foil. Cook at 375°F, mark 5, for 30 minutes.

Turn up the oven to 400°F, mark 6, and roast the lamb in one or two roasting pans for 12–15 minutes on a shelf higher than the potatoes.

Remove it, and turn up the oven to 450°, mark 8. Roll the lamb in the seasoned breadcrumbs. Put the racks back in the roasting pan and pat any remaining crumbs onto the surfaces. Drizzle 1–2 ounces of melted butter over it and cook the lamb for a further 10–15 minutes.
Remove the paper from the potatoes for the last 10 minutes so that they brown slightly. The lamb should be pink inside and the crumbs golden.

Slice the lamb, place the cutlets symmetrically on top of the potatoes, garnish with watercress and serve.

EDITOR'S NOTE: this is a difficult dish to time, since ovens vary greatly in their reaction to changes.

Spiced pears

Pengethley Hotel, Ross-on-Wye
chefs: Mrs T. Harvey and Fraser Carruth

8 cooking pears
4 fl oz water
10 oz granulated sugar
6 fl oz dry cider
squeeze of lemon juice
¼ teasp cinnamon
2 cloves
strip of orange rind
juice of half lemon
whipped cream

Choose a small, deep pan in which the pears can stand upright. In it dissolve the sugar in the water and bring to the boil.

Peel the pears, leaving them whole, with their stalks on. Put them straight into the sugar syrup to prevent their discolouring. Add the cider, the squeeze of lemon juice, the spices and the peel, cover the pan tightly and simmer very gently until the pears are tender but not over-soft. (This will vary greatly with the size and variety of pear.)

Put the pears in a small, deep serving dish, still upright. Strain the juice, take enough of it to cover the pears and boil it up with the juice of the half lemon. Pour this syrup over the pears and chill them thoroughly. Serve them with whipped cream.

EDITOR'S NOTE: this may be made the day before. The pears do not discolour, even if they are not entirely covered by the syrup, as long as the dish is securely covered. The extra syrup could be used on fruit salad or with baked apples. If you prefer, the pears can be cooked in the oven in an earthen-ware casserole.

Spring menu 7

pigeon casserole with celery and walnuts

red cabbage or red cabbage salad

orange and lemon charlotte (8)

If you invite people back for supper after the theatre or a film, you want dishes which can be served quickly and which are not so heavy that your guests spend a sleepless night afterwards. You also want to be able to talk while the meal is being prepared. The supper menu here satisfies all those points and is also pleasantly out-of-the-way. The pigeons are served in a coffee-coloured wine-and-cream sauce. The celery and walnuts give texture and colour contrast. The red cabbage, suitable for most game, is particularly convenient here because it can be reheated without spoiling. The sweet, although light, is a formal 'set-piece' with a welcome fresh flavour to end the evening in style.

Since the pigeon casserole reheats well, it seems wiser to make it earlier in the day, or even the day before. If you are serving the cabbage hot, it can also be prepared beforehand and reheated. As a salad – slightly less digestible – it could be shredded ahead of time and kept crisp and cool in a plastic bag so that you have only to add chopped apple, sultanas, parsley and a dressing, either vinaigrette with a little brown sugar in it or mayonnaise, before serving. If some of your guests are certain to be hungry, you might decide to serve rice or barley (cooked pilaff fashion) as well. The orange and lemon charlotte can also be prepared the day before.

Wine suggestions

MAIN COURSE	EITHER	OR
	white Hermitage	Côte de Beaune burgundy (Volnay, Beaune, Pommard)

The dry Hermitage (which could be used in the casserole) will contrast with the slight sweetness of the pigeon and cabbage; it improves with age. The heavier red burgundy would do if you wanted a closer match. The white wine could also be sipped as an aperitif.

Pigeon casserole with celery and walnuts

Leith's, London   chef: Antonio Lopez

4 pigeons
1½ oz butter
2 small rashers streaky bacon
6 stalks celery
2 oz shelled walnuts
1 dessertsp flour
7 fl oz dry white wine
7 fl oz stock (page 170, 171)
bouquet garni (page 168)
salt, pepper
1½ tablesp double cream

Wash the pigeons, inside and out, and pat them dry.

Melt half the butter in a heavy frying-pan. Chop the bacon and fry it slowly in the butter for 3 or 4 minutes. Remove it to a large, ovenproof casserole. Brown the pigeons in the butter and bacon fat.

Put them in the casserole, breast side down, and in the fat fry the chopped celery and walnuts until just turning colour, adding the remaining butter if necessary. Stir in first the flour, then the wine and stock and bring to the boil, stirring constantly. Pour the sauce over the pigeons and sink the bouquet garni in the sauce. Season. Cover the casserole with its lid, using foil or grease-proof paper to seal it if necessary.

Put the casserole in a slow oven (325°F, mark 3) until the pigeons are tender. This should take about 3 hours but very old birds may take longer and more stock would have to be added during the cooking.

Remove the pigeons to a serving platter. Skim any fat off the sauce and remove the bouquet garni. If the sauce is too thin, reduce it by rapid boiling. Stir in the cream and spoon the sauce over the pigeons.

Red cabbage

Gravetye Manor, East Grinstead   chef: Karl Loderer

1 medium-sized red cabbage
2 medium-sized onions
2 cooking apples
1 bay leaf
salt, pepper
2 or 3 smoked bacon rinds
ham knuckle or bone, if available
2 tablesp redcurrant jelly
2 tablesp white wine vinegar
2 tablesp red wine

Shred the cabbage finely; chop the onions; peel, core and slice the apples. Put them in layers in a casserole, adding seasoning between the layers. Bury the bay leaf, bacon rinds and bone in the middle. Heat the redcurrant jelly in the vinegar and wine and pour it over. Cover the casserole with a tight-fitting lid and cook in a slow oven (300°F, mark 2) for 2 to 3 hours. Stir it occasionally. Remove the bay leaf, rinds and bone before serving.

EDITOR'S NOTE: red cabbage can be made the day before and reheated. A pinch of powdered cloves is an interesting addition to this dish.

Orange and lemon charlotte (8)

The Elms Hotel, Abberley
chef: Mrs A. Schädler

24–32 sponge fingers or boudoir
   biscuits
2 tablesp rum
$\frac{1}{4}$ lb butter
$\frac{1}{4}$ lb caster sugar
3 eggs
grated rind and juice of
   one large orange
grated rind and juice of 1 lemon
1 pinch grated nutmeg
$\frac{1}{2}$ pint double cream
large pinch cream of tartar

Line the base and sides of a 7-inch straight-sided mould with buttered paper or foil. Sprinkle the sponge fingers with rum. Cut some of them diagonally and fit them into the bottom of the mould in a star shape with the sugared side downwards. Then pack about 16–20 fingers upright round the side of the mould with their sugared side facing outwards.

Cream together the butter and sugar. Separate the eggs, and whisk the yolks until they are creamy. Beat them into the mixture. Stir in the grated rinds of orange and lemon, and slowly add the juice. Flavour with a little nutmeg. Whisk the cream until it is thick, then stir it into the mixture. Whisk the egg whites with a pinch of cream of tartar until they are stiff, then fold them into the rest of the mixture.

Pour it into the lined mould and cover the top with the rest of the sponge fingers, shaped to fit. Sprinkle with more rum. Freeze in a deep freezer for $2\frac{1}{2}$ hours, or in the ice compartment of the refrigerator for 8 hours, or overnight.

Allow to thaw a little for half an hour before serving. Turn it onto a flat plate and remove the buttered paper or foil.

Summer menu 1

chachouka *or* **ratatouille**

involtini alla casareccia, boiled potatoes, broad beans

strawberry pots de crème *or* **fraises Charles Stuart**

Such a flamboyant menu, using dishes of mixed nationalities, perhaps calls for guests to match. The style is eclectic rather than classic, but the meal should appeal to most people who enjoy new flavours. It is not one to inflict on the conservative eater, since even the strawberries which belong with a proper English June appear in disguise.

Both first courses are made by gently stewing mixed vegetables: chachouka combines onions, tomatoes and green peppers, with a baked egg in the centre for fun and decoration; ratatouille adds aubergines, courgettes and garlic to those vegetables and, unlike the other, can be served hot or cold. If you wish to have a simpler first course, a tomato salad, with basil or marjoram and vinaigrette, would fit in well.

The involtini are veal escalopes rolled round a stuffing of cheese, sage and garlic, with a red wine and marsala sauce. These rich flavours need only the plainest of vegetables and the potatoes and beans make a colour contrast as well. Plain boiled noodles could be substituted for the potatoes.

Both sweets use strawberries, neither of them 'au naturel'. If you find magnificent berries, you may think it a shame to mess them about at all. In that case, serve them with some cream and relax. With less-than-perfect fruit, or for a change if you are lucky enough to have had a glut of them, try the little pots de crème (an orange flavour goes particularly well with strawberries), or fraises Charles Stuart, where the berries are lightly cooked with orange segments and flavoured with Drambuie. If there are no strawberries available, you could make gosebery tarte (page 166) or Cold Love (page 100), both of which take advantage of other seasonal fruit.

Chachouka and hot ratatouille will require some last-minute attention, and the veal too has to be cooked just before dinner. However, since the sweet can be prepared a long way ahead and the vegetables are simple, your schedule need not be too demanding, as long as all possible preparation is done ahead. You need not supervise the veal for its entire cooking period but it does require frequent turning, and you must be prepared to look at it every five minutes or so.

Wine suggestions

MAIN COURSE

EITHER	OR
Chianti Classico	Rioja

Either match the wine to dish with a really good Chianti, or switch nationalities with a Spanish Rioja, available in all price-ranges and qualities.

Timetable

THE DAY BEFORE — Prepare fraises Charles Stuart or strawberry pots de crème.

ON THE DAY

2¼ hours before dinner	Ratatouille – prepare vegetables.
1½ hours before	Chachouka – prepare vegetables.
1¼ hours before	*either* Cook ratatouille.
	or Cook chachouka vegetables.
¾ hour before	Fraises Charles Stuart – put in goblets and decorate.
½ hour before	Start cooking involtini.
¼ hour before	Put potatoes and beans on to cook.
	Chachouka – fill dishes with the vegetables.
10 mins before	Chachouka – add the eggs and bake.
just before	Take chachouka from oven, reduce temperature and put involtini to keep hot in their serving dish.

Chachouka

Houstoun House, Uphall
This is a Tunisian dish, prepared by the proprietor (Keith Knight) or one of his assistants:
William, Bill and Willie.

2 medium-sized onions
2 tablesp cooking oil
1½ lb tomatoes, fresh or tinned
3 green peppers
salt
Tabasco or cayenne
pinch of sugar
4 eggs

Slice the onions finely. Heat the oil and cook them in it gently until they have softened. If fresh tomatoes are used, scald and peel them; if tinned, drain them. Chop the tomato flesh roughly and add it to the onions. Seed and slice the green peppers and add them. Season.

Cover the pan and simmer gently for an hour, removing the lid for the last five minutes to allow some of the liquid to evaporate.

Butter four ovenproof dishes and cover the bottom with a layer of the vegetables. Make a well in the centre and break an egg into each one. Bake in a moderately hot oven (375°F, mark 5) for about 10 minutes or until the eggs have set.

As a variation, the eggs can be scrambled separately and added just before serving.

Ratatouille

L'Etoile, Edinburgh
chef: Jean-Marc Bordeau

2 aubergines
3 courgettes
2 medium-sized onions
2 green peppers, or 1 green and
   1 red
4 or 5 tomatoes
¼ pint olive oil
2 cloves garlic
salt, pepper
parsley
fresh basil

Slice the unpeeled aubergines and courgettes, sprinkle them with salt and leave them to drain for an hour covered with a weighted plate.

Slice the onions. Seed the peppers and peel the tomatoes; cut them all into slices. Fry the onions in the oil until slightly coloured; add the chopped garlic, the peppers, aubergines and seasoning. Let them simmer gently in a covered pan. Ten minutes later add the courgettes and

tomatoes and continue to stew gently for ¾ hour. Remove the lid and give it another 10 minutes to dry a little. Alternatively, the ratatouille may be cooked in a moderate oven (350°F, mark 4) for about an hour.

Serve either hot or cold.

EDITOR'S NOTE: ratatouille may also be served as a vegetable with a plain roast, or grilled meat or chicken.

Involtini alla casareccia

Pool Court Restaurant, Pool-in-Wharfedale
chef: David Armstrong

8–12 escalopes of veal
¾ teasp chopped fresh sage
1 large clove garlic
1 oz grated Parmesan
1 oz grated Emmenthal or
    Gruyère
salt, pepper
seasoned flour
2 oz butter
2 tablesp Marsala
½ pint red wine

Trim any fat or skin from the escalopes and beat them as flat and thin as possible between sheets of polythene or waxed paper, using a meat bat or rolling pin.

Mix together the sage, crushed garlic, both cheeses, salt and pepper. Spread about one heaped teaspoonful on each escalope, roll it up and secure the end with a cocktail stick. Then dip these rolls in seasoned flour. Heat the butter in a frying-pan and sauté them on all sides to seal the meat. Transfer to a second frying or sauté pan, or a flame-proof dish.

Deglaze the first pan with the Marsala, scraping up the residue with a wooden spoon. Add the red wine and let it bubble for a few moments. Strain it over the escalopes and leave them to simmer gently, uncovered, for 15–20 minutes.

The sauce, which should barely cover them at first, will gradually reduce and thicken by the end. Turn the escalopes from time to time in the sauce to prevent them from getting too dry. Check the seasoning.

Strawberry pots de crème

Sharrow Bay Hotel, Ullswater
chef/proprietor: Francis Coulson

½ lb fresh strawberries
½ pint double cream
4 dessertsp caster sugar
2–3 dessertsp orange curaçao
    or Cointreau
3 large or 4 small egg yolks

Liquidise the strawberries or rub them through a sieve. Scald the cream and stir into it the sugar and liqueur. Blend in the pureed strawberries. Taste to see if more liqueur is needed to add 'bite'.

Whisk the egg yolks until they are thick and creamy. Pour the strawberry cream onto them and whip the mixture lightly. Pour it through a sieve (if the fruit has not already been sieved) into four medium-sized ramekins or ovenproof dishes, and place these in a bain-marie (page 168).

Cover the whole dish with foil and poach the pots in the centre of a slow oven (300°F, mark 2) until they are firm – about half an hour. Keep a sharp eye on them as they will curdle if they are allowed to boil.

Chill and serve decorated with a fresh strawberry and a swirl of whipped cream.

Out of season, this dessert could be made with tinned or frozen strawberries but the result would be less delicious.

Fraises Charles Stuart

The Nare Hotel, Veryan
chef: Leslie Mortimer

1 lb fresh strawberries
4 or 5 oranges
2 oz granulated sugar
¼ pint Cornish cream
3 tablesp Drambuie
a few angelica leaves

Wash the strawberries. Peel two oranges and divide them into segments; if these are large, cut them in half. Put the juice of the other two oranges into a pan with the strawberries, oranges and sugar. Simmer the fruit gently for ten minutes or so. If there is not enough liquid, add more orange juice, or a little water. When the fruit is cooked, add the liqueur and leave to cool a little before chilling.

Spoon the fruit into goblets and decorate it with whipped Cornish cream and angelica leaves.

Summer menu 2

fresh grapefruit and crab salad *or* **salade niçoise**

steak à la moutarde *or* **tournedos Médicis, mange-tout peas** *or* **asparagus**

apricot torte with almonds (6), *or* **cheese**

This meal is ornate enough for a special occasion. Since it is also rather light, except for the sweet, you might choose to serve it when you are going with friends to a theatre or concert, with the first two courses beforehand and the handsome sweet afterwards with coffee and a leisurely liqueur. There are many advantanges to this kind of split meal: the hostess is not exhausted by prolonged effort, the guests are not so overfed that they fall asleep in the middle of the play, and there is an excuse to talk the evening over afterwards in comfortable surroundings.

If you choose the first salad, remember that the point is the *fresh* grapefruit, *fresh* crab and *fresh* (i.e. home-made) mayonnaise. Salade niçoise, the alternative, uses tinned tuna and anchovies (which lose little by this method of preservation) with French beans, cucumber and tomatoes in vinaigrette.

There is a choice of sauces for your steak in these two recipes, both simple, classic and delicious. Steak à la moutarde is cooked with cream, brandy, white wine and mustard, to produce a honey-coloured sauce flecked with parsley. Tournedos Médicis has red wine, port and cream for its sauce, with rosemary as a herb; the result is a speckled pink sauce rather like the Marsala one often served with veal. Choose this one if you like a sweet undertone, the mustard sauce for a little more bite. Either would look and taste well with the delicate green vegetables.

The apricot torte is worth coming home to, with its rich pastry base and handsomely-glazed filling, flavoured with kirsch and decorated with almonds.

If you make the pastry the previous day and the filling for the torte on the morning of the party, you will then have only the salads to prepare beforehand and the steaks to cook just before you sit down to dinner.

Wine suggestions	MAIN COURSE	EITHER	OR
		A good claret (St. Estèphe, e.g. Ch. Cos-d'Estournel; St. Emilion, e.g. Ch. Pavie)	A good burgundy (Vosne-Suchots, Volnay-Caillerets)

This is entirely a matter of taste. Buy the best of whichever you can find and afford.

	DESSERT	EITHER	OR
		A good Barsac (Ch. Coutet, Ch. Climens)	Asti Spumante

Particularly if you follow our suggestion and have dessert on its own after the theatre, a glass of wine would be welcome. The Barsac is rich and honeyed, the Asti tastes of Muscat grapes and sparkles. The Asti will be cheaper and easier to find. Serve either chilled.

Timetable	THE DAY BEFORE	Apricot torte – make pastry.
	ON THE DAY morning	Apricot torte – complete the preparation. Grapefruit and crab salad – cook and shell crab if necessary; make mayonnaise.
	1¼ hours before dinner	*either* Make salade niçoise and chill *or* Make grapefruit and crab salad.
	1 hour before	Steak à la moutarde – season steaks.
	20 mins before	Asparagus – start cooking (if it is young it will take less time).
	12–15 mins before	Cook steak à la moutarde.
	10 mins before	Cook tournedos Médicis.
	5 mins before	Cook mange-tout peas.

Fresh grapefruit and crab salad

Ardnagashel House, Bantry
chef: Mrs Kaulback

¾ lb fresh, cooked crab
4 sticks celery
2 grapefruit
salt, pepper
¼ pint mayonnaise (page 171)
lettuce

Break the crab into pieces. Dice the celery. Peel the grapefruit, remove all pith and cut the flesh into segments. Put some aside for decoration. Fold the crab and celery into the mayonnaise and add seasoning.

Then add the grapefruit segments and toss lightly.

Line a dish with a bed of lettuce, cover with the salad and garnish with grapefruit segments.

Salade niçoise

Romans, Silchester
chef: Louis Bielski

1 lb whole French beans
½ oz butter
¼ cucumber
2 large or 3 small tomatoes
6 anchovy fillets
about 12 black olives
small can tuna fish (about 3½ oz)
vinaigrette (page 172)
garlic
lettuce

Cook the beans in a little salted water and the butter until tender but still firm. Drain them and allow them to cool. Slice the cucumber thinly without peeling it. Skin, seed and quarter the tomatoes. Leave the anchovy fillets whole; stone the olives if necessary. Break up the tuna fish into manageable pieces.

Toss all these ingredients in the vinaigrette, well seasoned with garlic, and chill. Just before serving, arrange the salad on a bed of lettuce.

Steak à la moutarde

Au Fin Bec, London
chef: G. Gensale

4 thick fillet steaks
2 cloves garlic
salt, pepper
2–3 oz butter
4 tablesp dry white wine
2 tablesp brandy
1–2 teasp Dijon mustard
1 dessertsp chopped parsley
¼ pint double cream

Rub the steaks all over with the cut garlic. Season them with salt and pepper. Fry in the hot butter to the desired degree. Remove the steaks and keep them hot.

Rinse the pan with the white wine, scraping up the residue with a wooden spoon. Add the brandy and the mustard and stir well to blend them. Add the parsley and cream and stir over the heat until the sauce is hot but not boiling. Pour it over the steaks and serve.

Tournedos Médicis

Le Carrosse, London
chef: G. Borzoni

4 thick fillet steaks
1 oz butter
fresh rosemary
4 tablesp red wine
4 tablesp port
4 tablesp double cream
salt, pepper

Sauté the tournedos in the butter with a few sprigs of fresh rosemary until cooked to your liking. Remove the steak to a warm dish and discard the rosemary.

Add the wine and port to the pan and stir and scrape to incorporate all the pan juices. Boil rapidly until the liquid is reduced by about a third. Add the cream, boil for a few minutes more, and season the sauce to taste. Pour it over the steaks and serve immediately.

Apricot torte with almonds (6)

Country Fare, Buckfastleigh
chef: John Stewart

for the Vienna pastry base
¼ **lb unsalted butter**
3 oz caster sugar
2 small eggs
2 drops almond essence
2 drops vanilla essence
6 oz flour
¼ **oz ground almonds**

for the filling
2 lb fresh apricots or 2 1-lb
  tins of apricot halves
¼ **lb vanilla sugar (page 169)**
½ **pint water**
1 tablesp kirsch

for decoration
16–18 split almonds
2 tablesp apricot jam
½ **oz flaked almonds**

To make the base, blend together (without creaming) the softened butter, sugar, eggs and essence with a wooden spoon or a beater. When it is well blended, add the flour and ground almonds all at once and mix quickly and gently into a dough. Form it into a ball, flour it lightly, wrap it in greased paper and put it in the bottom of the refrigerator for an hour.

Butter and flour an 8-inch flan case and roll out or press the pastry by hand to fit the base. (Keep everything as cool as possible and dust the pastry generously with flour while rolling out.) Press the edge of the pastry against the side of the flan ring to raise it slightly, then even it with a fork or pastry cutter. Place the case on a baking sheet and bake in a fairly hot oven (400°F, mark 6) for 15–20 minutes. When it is a good light brown, remove it from the case and cool it on a wire rack.

If you are using fresh apricots, clean, halve and stone them. Bring the sugar and water to the boil and poach them gently – do not over-cook them. Lift out about 16 to 18 halves and continue to cook the remainder until they are very soft. If tinned apricots are being used, select firm halves and cook the rest in their own syrup with a piece of vanilla pod. When these apricots are soft, drain them and rub them through a sieve. Reduce the syrup until it is fairly thick. Add the kirsch and one or two tablespoonsful of the syrup to the pureed apricots to thin it just a little.

Spread the puree over the base right to the edge. Skin the reserved halves and arrange them on top of the puree. Toast some split almonds lightly under the grill and place one on top of each apricot.

Make a glaze by melting the apricot jam with a tablespoonful of the left-over syrup and brush this all over the top and sides of the torte. Toast the flaked almonds – broken up a little so that they will adhere more easily – and press then round the sides of the torte with a knife. Serve with whipped or pouring cream, if you wish.

Summer menu 3

smoked haddock croquettes with sauce tartare *or* **gazpacho**

caneton aux olives, fresh green peas, new potatoes

raspberry Pavlova (4–6) *or* **gooseberry meringue tart (4–6)**

Guests who are particularly interested in food and cooking would enjoy this meal with a savoury beginning and fruity finale. After the effort involved in preparing the hot first course (if you choose the croquettes) you can relax and enjoy the rest of the meal with everyone else, since there is no carving to be done and very little last-minute garnishing.

The deep-fried croquettes are made of haddock and creamed potato. Serve them with sauce tartare, as the restaurant suggests, since its cold sharpness is a foil for the smoked haddock's savoury richness. If it is a hot day or if the frying smells are likely to carry into your dining-room, you might prefer to serve gazpacho, the cold Spanish soup made with fresh tomatoes and colourfully garnished with croûtons and chopped vegetables.

The recipe for caneton aux olives is an adaptation of the more common one, and works very well in the domestic kitchen. The joints of duck are cooked in a brown, wine-flavoured stock, with pimento-stuffed olives added towards the end of the cooking period. Obviously only simple vegetables are needed here.

Raspberry Pavlova (rumoured to be Australia's national dish) uses a large meringue shell as a base for whipped cream and fresh raspberries. If raspberries are not in season, or if you prefer a 'real' pie with pastry, choose the gooseberry meringue tart, at its best with fresh fruit.

The meringue shell for Pavlova, or the flan case of the tart, can be made a day ahead, but the Pavlova should be completed no more than an hour before dinner so that the meringue stays crunchy. The gazpacho and the tart can be made some hours before dinner, and the initial preparations for the haddock croquettes can also be carried out well ahead. The duck will be safely in the oven for its final cooking period by the time the guests arrive, so that after their arrival you will need only about 15 minutes to fry the croquettes or five to garnish the gazpacho.

Wine suggestions

	APERITIF AND FIRST COURSE	EITHER	OR
		Traminer	dry vermouth or sherry

The spicy Traminer would be a more adventurous choice, sherry or vermouth safer. All should be served chilled.

	MAIN COURSE	EITHER	OR
		Chilean claret	Provençal (Bandol)

Both wines are unusual. The Chilean wines are remarkably well-made – and cheap; the Provençal reds are light and interesting, but not always easy to find. If neither is obtainable, a St Emilion claret would naturally do.

Timetable

	THE DAY BEFORE	*either* – Gooseberry meringue tart – make pastry *or* – Raspberry Pavlova – make meringue shell.
	ON THE DAY morning	Gooseberry meringue tart – complete preparation. *either* Make gazpacho and chill it; prepare garnishes *or* Prepare haddock croquettes for frying and rest them in the refrigerator. Make tartare sauce.
	2 hour before dinner	Joint duck. Make stock.
	1 hour 40 mins before	Pre-heat oven for duck.
	1 hour 25 mins before	Put duck joints in oven for 25 minutes. Pavlova – whip the cream.
	1 hour before	Take duck from oven and put in a warmed casserole. Reduce oven temperature. Make the sauce.
	40 mins before	Put duck with sauce in the oven. Croquettes – coat with egg and breadcrumbs. Pavlova – complete the preparation.
	½ hour before	Haddock croquettes – heat deep fat. Prepare and cook potatoes, and keep them hot.
	20 mins before	Check the duck and reduce heat if necessary.
	¼ hour before	Fry croquettes.
	10 mins before	Cook peas.
	just before	Duck – add olives to sauce. Garnish gazpacho.

Smoked haddock croquettes

Box Tree Restaurant, Ilkley
chef/proprietors: Mr Reid and Mr Long

smoked haddock – 12 oz when
   skinned and boned
¼ pint milk
bouquet garni (page 168)
½ lb potatoes
2 oz onions
3 oz butter
cream
chopped parsley
2 eggs
salt, pepper
flour
home-made dried breadcrumbs
oil
sauce tartare (page 171)

Poach the haddock in the milk with a bouquet garni for about 10 minutes. Cook the potatoes in salted water. Chop the onion very finely and cook it gently in an ounce of butter until it is soft and transparent. Cream the potatoes with the remaining 2 ounces of butter and a little cream, salt and pepper. Mix together the fish, potatoes and onion. Add the parsley and one well-beaten egg; season.

Form the mixture into croquette shapes – rolls, balls or flat cakes – flour them and refrigerate them until they are firm. Roll them in beaten egg and breadcrumbs.

Heat enough oil for deep frying until it reaches about 375°F, and put in as many of the croquettes as the pan will take. When they have turned an even golden colour – after 2 or 3 minutes – drain them on absorbent paper. Keep them warm while frying subsequent batches. Serve them with sauce tartare.

Gazpacho

Dulcinea, Weybridge
chef/proprietor: Longinos Benavides

6 ripe tomatoes
1 large and 1 small onion
1 large and 1 small green pepper
1 cucumber
4 small cloves garlic
2 tablesp chopped parsley
3 slices white bread, without
   crusts
2 tablesp white wine vinegar
2 tablesp olive oil
a few drops Tabasco
7 fl oz iced water
salt, pepper
1 hard-boiled egg

Here are two possible methods:
1. Chop together very finely 5 of the tomatoes, the large onion and large green pepper, half the cucumber, the garlic, parsley, and two of the slices of bread. Put all of these into a bowl and mix them together with the vinegar, olive oil, Tabasco and iced water. Let the mixture stand for about 20 minutes before rubbing it through a sieve. Add sufficient additional iced water to give the consistency of thin cream. Check the seasoning.

2. As an alternative, the soup can be made in a liquidiser by pureeing all the above ingredients. The tomatoes should be skinned and deseeded first. Chill well, or serve with an ice cube in each bowl. The remaining tomato, small onion, half cucumber, small green pepper and hardboiled egg are chopped up and put into separate bowls. The bread is diced, or fried as croûtons if preferred. These garnishes are handed round with the soup.

Caneton aux olives

Ardnagashel House, Bantry
chef: Mrs Kaulback

**1 duckling, about 3½ lb dressed
   weight**
salt, pepper

for the stock
the carcase and giblets
1 or 2 shallots or 1 small onion
bay leaf
sprig of thyme
a few parsley stalks
a few peppercorns
½ pint water

for the sauce
3 tablesp flour
½ pint dry white wine
24–30 olives stuffed with pimento

Carve the duckling into four – two breasts and two legs. Sprinkle the joints with salt and pepper and put them in a roasting tin in the middle of a moderate oven (375°F, mark 5) for 25 minutes, to crisp the skin and release some of the fat.

While they are roasting, make some stock with the carcase, giblets, some shallots or an onion, herbs and enough water to cover. Bring these to the boil, skim, partially cover the pan and leave the stock to simmer.

Remove the duck from the oven, reduce the heat to 300°F, mark 2, and put the pieces into a warmed casserole. Pour off nearly all the fat from the roasting tin and stir into the remainder two tablespoonsful of flour. Cook over a medium flame until the flour is a rich, dark brown, then blend in half a pint of the strained duck stock and the white wine and bring to the boil, stirring continuously. Adjust the seasoning and add any juices from the duck.

Pour the sauce over the duck in the casserole and put it back in the oven for 20 minutes. By this time the sauce should be simmering gently; if it is cooking too fast, reduce the oven heat to 275°F, mark 1. Cook for a further 40 minutes, adding the stuffed olives, halved crossways, halfway through.

Raspberry Pavlova (4-6)

Bay Horse Inn, Winton
chef: Sylvia Gilson

3 egg whites
pinch of salt
6 oz caster sugar
1 teasp cornflour
1 teasp white vinegar
½ pint double cream
1 lb fresh raspberries

Line an 8-inch sandwich tin with oiled greaseproof paper. Whisk the egg whites with salt until stiff. Beat in half the sugar; add the cornflour to the remaining sugar and fold it in with a metal spoon. Add the vinegar.

Put the mixture into the prepared tin and bake it for 1¼ hours at 250°F, mark ½. Turn out quickly onto a serving dish and peel off the paper. Leave to cool.

Whip the cream till stiff. Just before serving, cover the meringue with the whipped cream, pile the raspberries on top and dredge with caster sugar.

Gooseberry meringue tart (4-6)

Gerrans Bay Hotel, Gerrans
chef: Mrs H. Iddison

for the pastry
6 oz self-raising flour
¾ oz cornflour
¼ teasp salt
¼ lb margarine or lard
2–3 tablesp water

for the filling
1 lb gooseberries, fresh or tinned
4–6 oz sugar

for the glaze
½ lb demerara sugar
1 oz cornflour
1 oz butter
¾ pint gooseberry juice

for the meringue
2 egg whites
2 oz caster sugar

Line an 8-inch flan case with short crust pastry and bake it blind (page 173) in a moderately hot oven (375°F, mark 5).

Top and tail the gooseberries and cook them gently with 4–6 ounces of sugar – depending on their ripeness – until they are tender but not broken. (If tinned gooseberries are being used, omit the sugar and this period of cooking.) When they have cooled, drain them, keeping the syrup, and fill the flan case with the fruit.

Make a glaze by blending the demarara sugar, cornflour and butter with ¾ pint of the gooseberry syrup.

If there is not enough, make up the quantity with some other fruit juice. Heat this gently, stirring, until it thickens. Pour over the gooseberries.

Whisk the egg whites until they are stiff, add a teaspoonful of sugar and continue to whisk until they are very firm. Fold in the rest of the sugar. Cover the top of the tart with the meringue, so that it touches the pastry all round. Put it into a very slow oven (250°F, mark ½) to set.

After about an hour it should be firm and only slightly brown. Serve the tart cold.

Summer menu 4

prawn cocktail *or* **crab mousse**

coeur de filet de porc aux herbes, tomates provençale, sauté potatoes

ambroisie de pêches *or* **blackcurrant ice-cream**

When you know that friends enjoy familiar dishes rather than wild experiments or when you have to entertain acquaintances whose tastes you do not know at all it is wise to choose a menu which is neither freakish nor alarming. Here all the dishes are based on well-known themes, although there are a few unconventional embellishments. The expensive first course is balanced by more modest main course and sweets.

The prawn cocktail is a superior version of a much-abused dish, with fresh fruit and a sauce based on home-made mayonnaise. The lightly-jellied crab mousse is garnished with cucumber. Both these appetisers are cool, light and attractive; if you wish to serve something different, the same qualities would be found in one of the avocado mousses (pages 40 and 142).

The pork fillet is cut in little médaillons, seasoned with rosemary and fried. The pan juices are blended with brandy and cream to make the sauce. The creaminess of this dish contrasts well with the tomates provençale and sauté potatoes suggested by the restaurant.

Both these sweets make the most of seasonal fruit. The ambroisie de pêches combines peaches and bananas with shredded coconut and cream. The blackcurrant ice-cream is flavoured with cassis as well as the fruit and has a splendid dark burgundy colour. If neither of these appeals, a fresh fruit salad (not using any of the fruit in the prawn cocktail) would make another acceptable ending to the meal.

Although the pork will need 20 minutes' attention just before dinner, it is an easy dish to cook and will not leave you or the kitchen area smelling of the frying-pan. The vegetables can be cooked at the same time. Everything else can be prepared well ahead, although the ingredients for the prawn cocktail should not be combined until just before serving.

Wine suggestions

MAIN COURSE

EITHER   OR

red Hermitage   Côte Rôtie

These wines both come from the northern part of the Rhône vineyards. Both are full, sturdy wines capable of holding their own with the rich pork dish. Both improve with age; Côte Rôtie is probably easier to find, and is notable for its taste of raspberries. Rhône wines may throw a sediment and are best decanted.

Timetable

ON THE DAY

morning — Blackcurrant ice-cream – make and freeze.
Prawn cocktail – prepare ingredients, but do not combine them.
Crab mousse – cook and prepare crab if necessary.

2¼ hours before dinner — Make crab mousse and chill it (if you are freezing ice-cream at the time, the mousse will set very quickly; otherwise it may take up to 1½ hours).

1½ hours before — Make ambroisie de pêches and chill.

1¼ hours before — Peel potatoes and boil them until barely soft.

1 hour before — Prepare meat and leave while seasoning permeates.
Cut tomatoes for tomates provençale.

¾ hour before — Prawn cocktail – complete preparation.
Crab mousse – turn out and decorate.
Ambroisie de pêches – whip cream.

20 minutes before — Cook pork, tomatoes and potatoes, and keep them hot.

before the sweet — *either* Put finishing touches to ambroisie de pêches *or* to blackcurrant ice-cream.

Prawn cocktail

Howard Arms, Ilmington
chef/proprietor: W. T. Last

heart of a lettuce
12 slices cucumber
2 medium-sized tomatoes
½ Charentais or canteloup melon
2 slices fresh pineapple
1 lb shelled prawns
¼ pint mayonnaise (page 171)
¼ pint single cream
tomato puree
24 capers
parsley

Line each glass or dish with one or two leaves of lettuce, three slices of cucumber and three of tomato. Scoop out 16 balls or cut 16 cubes of melon. Cut the pineapple into 12 chunks. Divide the melon and pineapple among the four glasses and add a quarter of the prawns to each. Mix together the mayonnaise and the cream, and colour it with a little tomato puree. Stir in the capers. Pour the sauce over the prawns and sprinkle a little chopped parsley on top.

Crab mousse

Golden Cross, Wootton Wawen
chef: Mrs Day

1 oz powdered aspic
a few slices cucumber or stuffed olives
½ lb cooked crab meat, fresh or frozen
4 tablesp mayonnaise (page 171)
2 teasp powdered gelatine
4 fl oz double cream
salt, pepper
sherry
lettuce
cucumber or lemon

Dissolve the aspic in half a pint of hot water. Pour half into a wetted 6-inch mould. Float slices of cucumber and/or stuffed olive in the aspic as decoration. Chill for about half an hour.

Pound or flake the crabmeat. Mix into it the mayonnaise, the remaining aspic, the gelatine (dissolved in 2 tablespoonsful of hot water) and the cream. Add plenty of seasoning – and if wished, about a tablespoonful of sherry. Pour this mixture into the mould and return it to the refrigerator until set – up to 1½ hours.

To turn out the mousse, dip the dish first into a bowl of hot water for about 10 seconds. Decorate it, if you have not already done so, and surround it with lettuce and cucumber or lemon slices.

Coeur de filet de porc aux herbes

Le Français, London
chef: Jean-Jacques Figeac

1¼ lb pork fillet
salt, pepper
1 teasp crushed rosemary
2 tablesp cooking oil
2 tablesp brandy
2 fl oz double cream
parsley

Trim any fat off the fillet and cut it across at 1½-inch intervals to make about 20 thick médaillons. Sprinkle these on both sides with salt, coarsely ground black pepper and rosemary. (If the steaks are left for half an hour before cooking, these seasonings will have time to permeate.) Heat the oil in a frying-pan and cook the médaillons over a strong heat for 4 minutes on each side. Reduce the heat, cover the pan and give them a further 5 minutes on each side. Transfer to a serving dish and keep warm while making the sauce.

Deglaze the frying-pan with the brandy, scraping up the residue with a wooden spoon. Let it bubble a little before stirring in the cream. Simmer for a minute or two, then pour over the pork. Sprinkle over the sauce a little chopped parsley.

Tomates provençale

4 medium-sized tomatoes
salt, pepper
1 tablesp olive oil
1 clove garlic
chopped parsley
fresh white breadcrumbs

Cut the tomatoes in half and remove the seeds. Season them, and cook them gently, cut side downwards, in a little oil until they are fairly soft.

Transfer to a flameproof dish, cut side up, sprinkle each with a little chopped garlic and parsley and cover with breadcrumbs. Pour a little oil over each one and put the dish under the grill until the breadcrumbs are crisp.

Ambroisie de pêches

Ardnagashel House, Bantry
chef: Mrs Kaulback

3 large or 4 small peaches
2 bananas
2 tablesp caster sugar
1 tablesp fresh lemon juice
1 oz shredded coconut
whipped cream

Skin the peaches by plunging them into boiling water for a minute and then into cold water. Cut them into slices. Peel the bananas and slice them.

Sprinkle the sugar and lemon juice over the fruit and toss them all together. Chill in the refrigerator for half an hour at least.

Just before serving, mix in the shredded coconut and divide the fruit among four glasses.
Pipe or spoon whipped cream over the tops.

EDITOR'S NOTE: American tinned shredded coconut is particularly moist and full of flavour.

Blackcurrant ice-cream (6)

Christopher's, Brighton
chef: Christopher Goff

½ lb blackcurrants, fresh or frozen
¼ lb sugar
2 tablesp crème de cassis liqueur
½ pint double cream

Wash the blackcurrants, then simmer them gently with the sugar and cassis until they are soft. Leave them to cool before puree-ing them in a liquidiser. Sieve to remove the skins and seeds. Whip the cream slowly and as it thickens, gradually blend in the blackcurrant puree.

Turn the refrigerator to its lowest setting. Pour the ice-cream into a metal or plastic container with a lid or foil cover, and put it into the ice-making compartment. Every so often stir the ice, turning the frozen edges, which harden first, into the middle so that the texture of the ice is as smooth as possible. How long the ice-cream will take to freeze depends to some extent on the depth of the mixture in its container and also on the individual refrigerator.

Serve in glass dishes or coupes with a little cassis poured on top of each.

Summer menu 5

tortilla mimosa *or* **omelette Arnold Bennett**

fasulya, rice, jeryik

Mrs Langan's chocolate pudding (8–10)

This meal would suit a family celebration. The ingredients are easily identifiable, which encourages children, and the first two courses are light in fat and high in protein. Just as well, since Mrs. Langan has neither conscience nor calorie-counter and anyone with a weight problem would need the excuse of a birthday before embarking on even the first slice of her pudding.

The omelettes are both simple, but seldom met with outside restaurants: the Spanish one has a filling of asparagus spears, the English one, creamed smoked haddock. If you want to avoid last-minute cooking, or have a heavy hand with omelettes you could serve marinated kipper fillets (page 88) or Snaffles mousse (page 142) instead.

The treatment of lamb in the Turkish fasulya is interesting, since one has really a fat-free stew, with French beans, tomatoes and garlic providing the extra flavours. The salad is refreshingly cool by contrast: cucumber dressed with yoghourt, oil, garlic and mint. It is supposed to partner the fasulya but if your family dislikes yoghourt, you could do something simpler with the cucumber: lemon juice and a little sugar, perhaps.

Mrs Langan's chocolate pudding looks like a transfigured swiss roll – a light chocolate 'sponge' is rolled round thick dessert chocolate and whipped cream, both of which ooze out of the ends. There can be more cream on top if you are shameless or shapely. It ought to feed eight or ten, but do not count on any leftovers. If something lighter seems wiser, the spiced pears (page 47) would go down well.

Mrs Langan's chocolate pudding could be made on the morning of the party or some hours before dinner. The lamb cooks slowly and needs no last-minute preparation. This leaves only the omelettes to cope with after the guests arrive. If you choose Arnold Bennett, the filling can be prepared and kept hot for a little while.

Wine suggestions

		EITHER	OR
APERITIF AND FIRST COURSE		Austrian or Hungarian Riesling	white Graves (Ch. Olivier, Ch. Laville-Haut-Brion)

Many people find these Rieslings more enjoyable than the better-known Yugoslav; the same taste of the Riesling grape is detectable. Ch. Olivier and Ch. Laville-Haut-Brion are classified Graves and benefit from bottle age, whereas the Riesling should be drunk young. Chill.

	EITHER	OR
MAIN COURSE	Turkish red (Buzbag)	Bulgarian red (Melnik, Cabernet)

With the Turkish fasulya, it would be appropriate – and fun – to serve a Turkish or Bulgarian wine. Buzbag, praised for balance, breeding and bouquet by Allan Sichel, is closer to burgundy, whereas the Bulgarians are more like claret. If you fail to find either, you could try a red from Cyprus or Greece.

Timetable

ON THE DAY

morning	Make Mrs Langan's chocolate pudding.
2¾ hours before dinner	Fasulya – prepare ingredients.
2 hours before	Fasulya – pre-heat oven to 325°F, mark 3.
1¾ hours before	Fasulya – put in oven for about 2 hours.
1 hour before	Make jeryik and chill.
	Make filling for omelette Arnold Bennett.
20 mins before	Put stock on to boil for rice.
	Cook asparagus.
¼ hour before	Put rice on to cook.
5 mins before	Make four omelettes.
	Omelette Arnold Bennett – reheat filling.
	Melt butter for rice.
just before	Fill omelettes and serve immediately.
before main course	Pour melted butter over rice.

Tortilla mimosa

Andalucia Restaurant, Rugby
chef: Carlos Garcia Gamblor

9–12 **uncooked asparagus spears**
8–12 **eggs**
3 **oz butter**
salt, cayenne pepper

Cook the asparagus spears upright, in boiling salted water for 10–20 minutes, depending on their size and freshness. Drain them, cut them in half and toss them in a little butter.

Make four omelettes: heat ½ ounce butter in a small omelette pan until it is foaming, and pour in the eggs, lightly beaten with a pinch of salt and a dash of cayenne pepper. Leave for a few seconds before disturbing the mixture, then lift up the cooked egg from the pan with a fork and allow the unset egg to flow under-neath and round the edges, so that all is very lightly set as quickly as possible – it should take little more than half a minute.

Remove from the heat and place a quarter of the hot asparagus spears in the centre. Fold the omelette away from the handle of the pan. Tip the pan over onto the serving dish so that the omelette falls onto it. Keep it hot. Make three more omelettes as quickly as possible and serve immediately.

Omelette Arnold Bennett

Kildwick Hall, Kildwick
This is an adaptation by Michael Quinn of a recipe created for Arnold Bennett by Jean Baptiste Virlogeux, Grill Room chef at the Savoy during the 1920s.

6 **oz smoked haddock**
½ **pint milk**
peppercorns, bay leaf, parsley
8 **tablesp double cream**
salt, pepper
8–12 **eggs**
2 **oz butter**
parsley

Poach the haddock for 10 minutes in a little milk seasoned with pepper-corns, bay leaf, parsley stalks but no salt. Drain, skin and bone the fish.

Flake the haddock and mix it with the cream. Heat it gently in a small pan so that the fish and cream mix-ture is hot and the cream has thicke-ned a little. Check the seasoning.

Make four omelettes as described above, and fold them onto a serving dish. Cut a slit in the top of each and fill the centre with a spoonful of the creamed haddock. Decorate them with sprigs of parsley and serve immediately.

Fasulya

Bosphorus Restaurant, Penarth
chef/proprietor: N. Binbasilar

for the lamb
a 3–3½ lb leg of lamb
** (approx 2 lb meat)**
1 lb French beans
½ lb tomatoes, fresh or tinned
2 large onions
2 cloves garlic
1 tablesp tomato puree
salt, pepper
½ pint water (approx)

for the rice
½ lb long grain rice
1 pint chicken stock
2 oz butter

for the salad
¾ pint plain yoghourt
salt
2 cloves garlic
1 cucumber
1 tablesp olive oil
fresh mint

Cut the meat in small pieces, discarding all fat and sinew. Wash and slice the beans. Place both lamb and beans in a casserole, preferably a shallow earthenware one. Add the chopped tomatoes and onions with two cloves of garlic. Mix the tomato puree, salt, pepper and water and add to the casserole. Cover and cook in the oven at 325°F, mark 3, for 2 hours or until the meat is tender.

Wash the rice thoroughly. Bring the stock to the boil and in it simmer the rice until it has absorbed all the liquid (about 30 minutes). Melt the butter and pour it over the rice just before serving.

For the salad, called *jeryik*, mix the yoghourt with salt to taste and two crushed cloves of garlic. Skin the cucumber and chop it finely. Place it in a shallow serving dish, pour the yoghourt carefully over it, sprinkle on the olive oil, and decorate with chopped mint. Chill briefly before serving.

EDITOR'S NOTE: any variety of mint would be effective – spearmint is particularly good.

Mrs Langan's chocolate pudding (8-10)

Odin's, London
chef/proprietor: Peter Langan

6 large eggs
½ lb caster sugar
2 oz cocoa
12 oz Bourn ville chocolate
¾ pint double cream
½ pint single cream (optional)

Grease a swiss-roll tin approximately 13 inches by 8 inches by 1 inch. Line it with greaseproof paper, mitring the corners so that they fit neatly, and grease that. Whip the egg yolks in a large bowl until they thicken. Add the sugar and beat again till thick, but not white. Add the cocoa and mix thoroughly. Whip the egg whites until they are stiff but not dry, and fold them gently into the yolks and cocoa. Pour the mixture into the prepared tin. Bake at 350°F, mark 4, for 20 minutes, or until the mixture is set without being dried out. Allow the sponge to cool before turning it out onto a sheet of greaseproof paper lightly dusted with caster sugar.

Melt the chocolate with a little water over a gentle heat. Allow it to cool but not go solid. Pour the melted chocolate onto the sponge base.

Whip the double cream until thick, adding the single cream also if you wish extra for decorating. Spoon the cream over the chocolate and spread it evenly with a spatula.

Roll up the cake gently by moving your fingers under the greaseproof paper. When it is almost completely rolled up, tip it onto a serving plate with the seam down. Cover with the remaining cream, leaving the rolled ends visible, and decorate, if desired, with chocolate shavings.

EDITOR'S NOTE: Mr Langan points out that if this fragile, flour-free sponge breaks as you roll it, it looks very attractive with the cream and chocolate oozing out.

Summer menu 6

lemon soup *or* **cold curried apple soup**

darne de saumon de Médicis, salad

American cheesecake (6) *or* **Italian cheesecake (6)**

This is a meal for a hot summer evening when you wish to feel as coolly elegant as your guests, and when you all want food that is demanding of neither the cook nor the digestion. Since the first and last courses are cold and the main one is also easy to serve and eat, you might decide to have dinner in the garden or on the patio.

Both soups can be served cold, but the lemon one, based on chicken stock and cream, is equally good hot, if the weather changes between choosing the menu and serving the meal. The curried apple soup is not 'hot' in any sense of the word, but the flavour of the curry complements the apples and cream very nicely. The soup is rather thick and a creamy gold colour with the watercress garnish for contrast.

The salmon is treated very simply, which is why the chef stresses that it should be fresh, with no experience of the deep-freeze. It is first grilled with a coating of breadcrumbs and then cooked briefly in the oven along with the tomatoes stuffed with béarnaise. If you are addicted to béarnaise, make the full quantity in the recipe on page 174 and serve the remainder separately. A mixed salad – no tomatoes – goes well with the rich fish and sauce.

The cheesecakes both have cream cheese as their main ingredient, but while the Italian one has a sponge base and is flavoured with raisins and lemon juice, the American one uses digestive biscuits, vanilla and sour cream. They are both easy to serve, as are gateau Fontes (page 42), raspberry Pavlova (page 66) or spiced pears (page 47).

The soups and sweets can be prepared either the day before the party or early on the actual day. You will then have nothing to do except stuff the tomatoes and grill the salmon at the last minute. If you decide to eat indoors, there will be no heavy cooking smells in the house to detract from the fresh, cool atmosphere you are trying to create.

Wine suggestions

MAIN COURSE

EITHER	OR
white burgundy	Loire
(Meursault, Corton-	(Vouvray)
Charlemagne)	

Corton-Charlemagne is rich, golden, expensive and hard to find; Meursault at its best is softer, but cheaper Meursaults can be harsh – so choose carefully. Vouvray varies from dry to medium sweet; the sweeter wines are long lived, the dry ones best drunk young. Do not overchill the burgundies.

Timetable

THE DAY BEFORE	Make either of the cheesecakes and chill overnight.
ON THE DAY	
morning	Cold curried apple soup – prepare and chill.
	Lemon soup – prepare. Chill if you decide to serve it cold.
1 hour before dinner	Prepare salad.
¾ hour before	Make béarnaise.
¼ hour before	Darne de saumon – prepare salmon, butter and crumbs.
5–10 mins before	Pre-heat oven for salmon.
	Grill salmon on one side for 5 minutes.
	Stuff tomatoes while salmon is grilling.
	Reheat lemon soup gently if you are serving it hot.
	Put salmon and tomatoes in oven.
last minute	Garnish cold curried apple soup.
	Add cream and chives to lemon soup.
between courses	Toss salad.

Lemon soup

Fantails, Wetheral
chef: M. Watson

½ pint béchamel sauce (page 174)
2 pints chicken stock (page 171)
salt, pepper
3 egg yolks
1–2 lemons
½ pint double cream plus a little
   whipped cream
chopped chives

Stir the stock into the béchamel and season with salt and pepper. Add the beaten egg yolks one at a time, and heat gently until the soup begins to thicken, stirring continuously. Do not let it boil. Flavour the soup with lemon juice. Start with the juice of one lemon and if the taste is not pronounced enough, add more – it must have a strong, lemony flavour.

Stir in the double cream, off the heat, and then reheat gently. Serve in bowls, topped with a spoonful of whipped cream and a sprinkling of chopped chives.

CHEF'S NOTE: this soup is also delicious chilled but then needs slightly more seasoning.

Cold curried apple soup

The Hat and Feather, Knutsford
chef: Mrs Stirling

1 tablesp butter
1 small onion
1 dessertsp curry powder
1½ pints chicken stock
1 dessertsp cornflour
2 lb dessert apples
juice of ½ small lemon
scant ¼ pint single cream
1 egg yolk
salt, pepper
watercress (or applemint)

Melt the butter, add the chopped onion and sweat it gently for a few minutes until the onion is soft but not brown. Stir in the curry powder and then the stock. Mix the cornflour with a little water to make a thin paste and add to the mixture, stirring. Simmer for 8 minutes.

Peel, core and slice the apples finely; add them with the lemon juice, and continue to simmer until the apples are soft (about 10 minutes).

Put the cream into a little pan to warm. Remove from the heat and beat in the egg yolk. Add the cream and egg mixture to the soup gradually, stirring. Remove from the heat immediately. Sieve or blend in a liquidiser. Season to taste. Cool, and chill in a refrigerator overnight.

Serve chilled, garnished with chopped apple and watercress or applemint.

Darne de saumon de Médicis

Royal Hotel, Comrie
chef/proprietor: Alastair M. Hood

4 fresh salmon steaks about
¾ inch thick
2 oz butter
2 oz fresh white breadcrumbs
salt, pepper
4 large or 8 small tomatoes
4–6 tablesp sauce béarnaise
(page 174)

Wipe the steaks with a damp cloth and dry them. Melt the butter, dip each steak into it, and then into the breadcrumbs. Season them with salt and pepper and place them in a flameproof dish (or failing this, on a foil-covered grill rack). Dribble any left-over butter over the steaks, or add a few knobs of fresh butter, and grill them under a hot grill for up to 5 minutes without turning them and until they are nicely browned.

While they are cooking, pre-heat the oven to 250°F, mark ½, and prepare the stuffed tomatoes. Stand the tomatoes stalk side downwards, and cut a slice off the top. Carefully scoop out all the flesh and seeds, then fill the shells with one or two spoonsful of sauce béarnaise.

Arrange the tomatoes round the salmon steaks in their dish and bake in the oven for 15 minutes. By this time the salmon should be cooked – check to see if the central bone is loose – and the tomatoes should have softened a little and their sauce turned golden.

The dish will keep for a while if the oven is turned down as low as it will go.

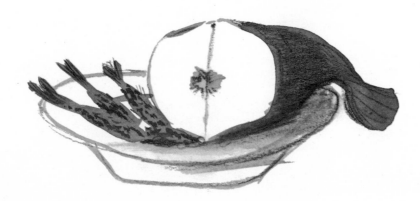

American cheesecake (6)

Central Hotel, Dover
chef/proprietor: Manfred Winands

for the base

¼ lb digestive (sweetmeal) biscuits
½ teasp cinnamon
½ teasp nutmeg
2 oz butter

for the filling

2 eggs
5 oz caster sugar
2 8-oz packets Philadelphia cream
   cheese
½ teasp vanilla essence

for the topping

4 oz sour cream
2 oz caster sugar
few drops vanilla essence

Crumble the biscuits in a liquidiser or pound them to fine crumbs with a rolling pin. Mix in the spices. Melt the butter and stir it into the crumbs. Grease an 8-inch fairly deep-sided cake tin which has a removable base. Press the crumbs gently into a layer on the bottom of the tin and bake for 5–7 minutes in a fairly hot oven (400°F, mark 6). Leave to cool.

Make up the filling by whipping together the eggs and sugar until they are light and creamy. This is most easily done with an electric beater. Break up the cheese and add it gradually, continuing to beat until all the lumps have disappeared. Mix in the vanilla flavouring, then pour the filling onto the biscuit crust and return it to the oven, reduced to 375°F, mark 5, for 30–40 minutes, until the filling has set. Leave to get cold.

Whip together the sour cream, sugar and flavouring until it has the consistency of thick cream and then pour it carefully over the top of the cheesecake. Put in the refrigerator to set overnight or for at least 8 hours.

Italian cheesecake (6)

The White Dog Inn, Ewhurst
Pauline Collins, the chef, tells us that this recipe is from the Italian Alps

1 round sponge cake (slice of
   madeira or a flan case) to line tin
2 teasp gelatine
½ lb curd cheese
3–4 oz caster sugar
6 fl oz double cream
2 eggs
juice one small lemon
1–2 oz sultanas or raisins

Cut the sponge to make a thin layer on the bottom of a loose-bottomed 7-inch cake tin.

Add a little water to the gelatine, and melt over hot water, stirring carefully. Cool. Mix the cheese, sugar cream, egg yolks and lemon juice, and beat until smooth. (This may be done with an electric mixer.) Add the melted gelatine and mix well. Whisk the egg whites until stiff, and fold them into the cheese mixture. Fold in the sultanas and pour the mixture into the tin on top of the sponge.

Refrigerate for several hours, or overnight. Before serving, carefully remove the sides of the tin, leaving the cake on the base.

Summer menu 7

salmon pâté *or* **Oak House pâté**

American chicken salad, tomatoes

orange curd cream *or* **fruit and cheese**

This menu will make a lovely picnic, if you wish to have an elegant one for a special occasion rather than the more rugged cheese-sandwich-and-bottle-of-pop-in-the-pocket kind appropriate to hiking and casual family jaunts. Even if you never go to Glyndebourne or to a race meeting or out in a punt on Cam or Cher, you might find this a very enjoyable way to entertain in the summer. Since the meal would be just as good eaten at home, you are not at the mercy of the weather, as you would be if you had planned a barbecue. You will need plates, cutlery and glasses, but nothing requires carving or complicated manoeuvring by either the hostess or the guests.

The salmon pâté is gentle and creamy, the Oak House one much stronger with its flavours of chicken livers, garlic and brandy. The salad combines cold roast chicken strips with celery, grapes, apples and nuts in mayonnaise. The fresh oranges in the curd cream make a tangy mousse.

Everything can be prepared ahead of time. The salad and the sweet are nicer if served lightly chilled. If you do not have an insulated picnic bag, improvise as best you can with wide-mouthed thermos flasks, ice and thick wrappings. The pâtés and the orange curd cream could be set in small plastic cartons (yoghourt or cottage cheese empties) for easy transportation. Salad stuff should be carried separately in plastic bags and combined at the last minute with vinaigrette from a little screw-topped jar. Wholemeal bread (page 166) would go well with either pâté, but you my prefer rye or French if you are serving cheese.

Wine suggestions

EITHER	OR
A single-estate moselle from Bernkastel, Graach or Zeltingen	Portuguese vinho verde (e.g. Casal Garcia) or sparkling Saumur

You can taste the Riesling grape in both moselles and both 'fill the mouth'. The Portuguese vinho verde is drier, with a slight prickle; the Saumur, heavier and usually dry, is made by the champagne method and is relatively inexpensive. If river or lake is your only way of keeping the wine cool, Casal Garcia has the bonus of a handle for retrieving the bottle.

Salmon pâté

Crusoe Hotel, Lower Largo
chef: J. A. Crawford Horne

½ lb fresh salmon, cooked
½ medium-sized onion
¼ cucumber
4 egg yolks
¼ pint double cream
¼ pint béchamel (page 174)
salt, pepper
cucumber, lettuce

Remove any skin or bones from the salmon and flake it finely. Grate the onion and cucumber roughly and mix into the salmon.

Beat the egg yolks, stir the cream into them, then stir the mixture into the béchamel sauce. Season the sauce and combine it with the salmon. Butter a mould or a round pie dish, and fill with the mixture. Put into a bain-marie (page 168), cover, and cook in a moderate oven (325°F, mark 3) for 50 minutes or until firm. Remove and leave to cool.

When cold, turn out the pâté onto a dish and decorate with cucumber and lettuce.

Oak House pâté

Oak House Restaurant, Axbridge
chef/proprietor: C. H. Donovan

1 lb chicken livers
5 oz butter
1 small pinch mixed herbs
1 large pinch mixed spice
1 clove garlic
salt, pepper
2½ fl oz dry sherry
1 fl oz brandy

Clean the chicken livers and halve them. Sauté them for 2–3 minutes in 2 ounces of butter until they are stiffened but still pink inside. Add the herbs and spices, the garlic crushed with the salt, and the freshly ground black pepper. Remove from the heat and add the sherry and brandy.

You may either grind this mixture in a vegetable mill to obtain a fairly smooth pâté, or mash it with a fork for a rougher texture. Add the remaining butter, softened, and mix well.

Pack the pâté in individual dishes or a larger flat one. Serve with hot toast, or with French bread for a picnic.

EDITOR'S NOTE: chicken liver pâté, unbaked, as this is, is never a very attractive colour on its exposed surface. We suggest forking it up before serving.
This pâté mellows well and should rest in the refrigerator for at least 24 hours.

American chicken salad

The Rising Sun, St Mawes
chef: Leslie Slassor

a 2½-lb cooked chicken
½ pint mayonnaise (page 171)
4–6 sticks of celery
1 small onion
¼ lb green grapes
2 eating apples
2 oz shelled walnuts
2 oz shelled hazelnuts
lemon juice
fresh (chopped) or dried
  tarragon
salt, pepper
lettuce
whipped cream
watercress

Carve the chicken in long slices which can then be skinned and cut into strips. Make the mayonnaise with lemon juice rather than vinegar. Dice the celery and chop the onion finely. Halve the grapes and remove the pips. Core and slice the apples thinly, leaving the skin on. Break the nuts into two or chop them roughly.

Mix all these ingredients together in a bowl, adding the chicken last. Season the mayonnaise; add a little more lemon juice and some chopped tarragon. If it is too thick for coating the salad, lighten it with a little cream or water. Fold the mayonnaise lightly into the salad, taking care to cover all the apple to prevent its discolouring.

Put a bed of lettuce leaves on a flat dish and pile the salad on top. Decorate with a little whipped cream and watercress.

EDITOR'S NOTE: if your apples are a type which discolour quickly, slice them into a bowl of water with a little lemon juice in it. Dry the slices before adding them to the salad.

Orange curd cream

Carpenter's Arms, Eastling
chef: Mrs Nora Harvey

2 oranges
2 oz sugar
½ lb fresh curd cheese
¼ pint double cream

Peel and cut up the oranges and remove the pips. Put the flesh in the liquidiser with the sugar. Add the curd cheese and blend well. Add the whipped cream and blend again.

Put in individual glasses or dishes and chill for several hours.

This dish should be eaten the same day as it is made.

Autumn menu 1

Bell Inn smokies *or* **marinated kipper fillets**

steak and kidney pudding, marrow with curry sauce

apple and Stilton savoury *or* **cheese**

Few people have a song in their hearts when they think of traditional British cooking, but occasionally one has to defend the national honour by entertaining foreign visitors. It is a pleasure to be able to do it with dishes as good as these, which, if they are not all completely traditional, certainly incorporate characteristic elements or methods.

The smokies are flaked and cooked with tomatoes, cream and cheese, glazed to an attractive brown. Marinated kipper fillets are a good choice if you want to cut down on last-minute preparation, or on the expense of the meal.
If money can be forgotten, smoked salmon would be an ideal first course.

The steak and kidney pudding is not an elaborate dish, but has a superb gravy, and looks handsome in its napkin-wrapped basin. The marrow is only lightly curried, so that you will still have some palate left for wine.

The apple and Stilton savoury is refreshing, original and pretty, with its avocado-coloured filling of sieved Stilton and cream cheese inside dessert apples. You might prefer to have a selection of British cheeses with biscuits, oatcakes and bread, so that the wine can circulate till the end of the meal.

Since the only crucial piece of timing involved in preparing this meal is the last-minute glazing of the smokies, you should be able to take a drink with your guests before dinner, thus demonstrating typical British phlegm.

Wine suggestions

APERITIF AND FIRST COURSE	EITHER malt whisky	OR sherry (dry Oloroso, Amontillado)

It is difficult to generalise about malt whiskies, for each brand is distinctive. But as a rule, Highland malts (e.g. Glenlivet) are lighter, Island brews (e.g. Talisker from Skye) more peaty.

MAIN COURSE	EITHER Guinness, barley wine or dry still cider	OR red burgundy (Beaune, Pommard)

The first choices for this meal are British, the others more traditional.

LAST COURSE	EITHER Madeira (Bual, Verdelho)	OR late-bottled port

The Verdelho is drier than the Bual. If you decide on cheese, the port would be a better choice.

Timetable

THE DAY BEFORE	Marinated kipper fillets – put to marinate.
ON THE DAY morning	Bell Inn smokies – fillet smokies; prepare tomatoes. Prepare steak and kidney pudding.
3½ hours before dinner	Steak and kidney pudding – start cooking.
1½ hours before	Apple and Stilton savoury – prepare filling.
1 hour before	Marrow with curry sauce – prepare and cook.
¾ hour before	Marinated kipper fillets – complete the preparation. Bell Inn Smokies – preheat oven.
35 mins before	Bell Inn smokies – finish preparation; start cooking.
20 mins before	Apple and Stilton savoury – complete preparation.
just before	Glaze Bell Inn smokies.

Bell Inn Smokies

The Bell Inn, Aston Clinton
chef: Jakob Dick

4 small smokies
8 fl oz double cream
4 tomatoes
pepper
¼ lb grated cheese
(Parmesan or Gruyère)

Skin the smokies, remove all bones and flake the flesh. Put half the cream in a buttered, shallow earthenware dish. On this place the flaked fish. Blanch and skin the tomatoes and remove the seeds. Chop them roughly and spread over the fish. Season with pepper. Pour over the remaining cream. Sprinkle with cheese and bake at 350°F, mark 4, for 20 minutes.

Glaze briefly under a very hot grill.

Marinated kipper fillets

Bay Tree Hotel, Burford
chef: Miss Shann

8 kipper fillets
1 small onion
1 bay leaf

for the marinade
1 teasp caster sugar
1 teasp prepared mustard
3 tablesp white wine vinegar
4 tablesp olive oil
salt, pepper

for decoration
lemon slices
watercress

Skin the kipper fillets if necessary and arrange them in the bottom of a shallow dish. Cover them with the onion, cut into rings, and the bay leaf. Mix together the ingredients for the marinade and pour it over the fillets. Cover the dish and leave the fish in the marinade for 24 hours.

Drain the fillets and arrange them on a shallow dish. Garnish with lemon slices and watercress. Serve them with thin slices of brown bread and butter.

Steak and kidney pudding

Rules, London
chef: André Chion

for the filling
1½ lb stewing steak
½ lb ox kidney
1 medium-sized onion
¼ lb button mushrooms
½ teasp salt
pepper
1 tablesp chopped parsley

for the crust
½ lb plain flour
2 teasp baking powder
¼ lb suet
1 oz breadcrumbs
½ teasp salt
4–5 tablesp water

for the gravy
1 teasp Worcestershire sauce
½ pint water

Cut the trimmed steak and kidney into one-inch pieces. Chop the onion and mushrooms roughly and mix them with the meat, salt, pepper and chopped parsley.

Mix the dry ingredients for the crust together, and blend into them enough water to form a soft dough. Roll out three-quarters of the dough to a thickness of ¼-inch; grease a 2-pint pudding basin and line it with the dough, letting a little hang over the top edge. Fill the basin with the meat mixture and pour into it the water mixed with the Worcestershire sauce. Moisten the edge of the pastry and cover the top with the rest of the pastry, rolled to ¼-inch thickness.

Press the edges firmly together and trim off any excess. Cut a circle of greaseproof paper a little larger than the top, oil it and lay it face downwards on the pastry. Tie it round with string.

Steam the pudding in a covered steamer or saucepan half full of simmering water for at least 3 hours, and preferably 4, topping up with boiling water as it evaporates. The pudding will not spoil if cooked for longer; if time is limited, however, the steaming process can be reduced by partly cooking the meat the day before.

To serve, remove the paper, wrap a white napkin round the basin and bring it to the table.

Marrow with curry sauce

The French Partridge, Horton
chef/proprietor: D. C. Partridge

¼ lb onions
1 tablesp oil
1 clove garlic, crushed
1 teasp curry powder
¼ teasp allspice
a little sugar
2 tablesp tomato puree
salt, pepper
½ pint water
a 2–2½ lb marrow

Chop the onion and fry it gently in the oil until it is soft and transparent. Add all the other ingredients except the marrow and bring to the boil. Simmer for 15 minutes.

Peel the marrow and remove the seeds. Chop it into chunks and cook slowly in the sauce until it is just soft (about 15–20 minutes).

Apple and Stilton savoury

Swan House Hotel, Wilmcote
chefs: Jennifer Burton and Jennifer Newbold

6 oz Stilton
¼ lb cream cheese
salt, pepper
4 medium-sized dessert apples
vinaigrette (page 172)
1 lettuce

Rub the Stilton through a fine sieve. Mix the cream cheese into it and some salt and pepper.

Wash and polish the apples and cut a slice off the top of each. Carefully scoop out the flesh of each apple. Discard the cores but keep the rest. Chop it up and toss it in some

vinaigrette to prevent its discolouring.

Fill the apple shells with the cheese mixture and replace the tops.

Arrange them on a bed of lettuce surrounded by the chopped apple, and serve with extra vinaigrette.

Autumn menu 2

spinach soup *or* **tomato soup**

poulet au gratin à la crème landaise, rice, salad *or* **fennel** *or* **celery**

tarte aux pommes Joséphine (6)

Although this meal is relatively inexpensive, the dishes are interesting and particularly tasty. It would be hard to imagine any group of people who would not enjoy it, unless spinach still has school-dinner connotations for some. The strength of the soups is balanced by the delicacy of the chicken sauce, which in turn contrasts with the rich caramel in the apple tart.

The spinach soup is a smooth puree based on ham stock, with both flavours coming through clearly. It is rather heavier than the tomato soup with its fresh tomatoes and chicken stock. Both are decorated with cream; the tomato soup has sherry added too. Although you could substitute another favourite soup for either of these, it would be wise to avoid a creamy one which would look too similar to the chicken sauce. If you would prefer a cold first course, marinated kipper fillets (page 88) or orange and celery salad (page 127) could be served.

Poulet au gratin à la crème landaise (an adaptation of one of Elizabeth David's recipes in *French Country Cooking*) is a jointed chicken, simmered in a rich, meaty stock and served with a cream and mustard sauce. The completed dish is sprinkled with Parmesan and glazed quickly under the grill, so that it arrives at table very hot and golden crisp on top. Rice or creamed potatoes mop up the thin sauce; a salad including fennel, celery or chicory would go well with the chicken, as would the same vegetables cooked, should you prefer a hot side dish.

The sweet is an apple tart with several differences. The apples are cooked in caramel (worth trying instead of plain stewed apples even if you do not want to put them in pastry), decorated with peaches or cherries, and glazed with the remaining caramel. If something less sweet is wanted, hot fruit salad (page 114) or a compôte of lightly stewed fruit could be served instead.

Most of the preparation for this meal can be done on the morning of the party, and the soups and the pastry would not be harmed if made the night before. The stock for the chicken can be made as soon as you have jointed the bird, and the tart filling can be prepared on the morning of the party. This leaves only the final cooking and glazing of the chicken for the hour before dinner.

Wine suggestions

MAIN COURSE

EITHER
Pinot d'Alsace (also
called Tokay d'Alsace)

OR
red Graves (Ch. Pape-
Clément, Ch. Haut-Bailly)

The Pinot Gris grape produces a fresh dry wine,
easy to drink. But you may prefer to match the
sauce with a good red Graves. If this is a special
celebration, Ch. La-Mission-Haut-Brion would be
even better than the two above – and more expensive.

Timetable

THE DAY BEFORE

Spinach soup – make ham stock.
Tomato soup – make chicken stock.
Tarte aux pommes – make pastry case and bake.

ON THE DAY
morning

Poulet à la crème – joint chicken. Make stock.
Tomato or spinach soup – skim stock. Make soup.
Complete tarte aux pommes.

1 hour before dinner
50 mins before
$\frac{1}{2}$ hour before
$\frac{1}{4}$ hour before

Start cooking chicken pieces, except for the breasts.
Simmer chicken for 20 minutes.
Add chicken breasts. Continue to simmer.
Creamed potatoes – put potatoes on to boil.
Reheat soup.

10 mins before

Poulet – prepare sauce and pour it over chicken.
Keep hot.
Rice – start cooking.
Celery or fennel – put on to cook. Keep hot.

last minute

Tomato soup – add sherry and cream.
Spinach soup – add cream.

after first course

Brown the chicken quickly under the grill.
Creamed potatoes – prepare quickly.
Toss salad.

Spinach soup

Old Howgate Inn, Wester Howgate
chef: Mrs W. R. Garrad

½ lb leaf spinach
2 pints ham stock
1½ oz beef dripping or butter
1½ oz plain flour
nutmeg, pepper
cream

Wash the spinach and discard the toughest stalks. Put it in the stock, which should have had any fat removed previously. Bring to the boil and simmer for 2–3 minutes to cook the spinach.

Make a roux (page 169) from the dripping and flour, gradually stir in some of the stock, and then return all to the pot in which the stock and spinach were simmered. Cook gently for a few minutes, stirring frequently. Put it in the liquidiser and blend till smooth (or sieve).

Reheat the soup, seasoning to taste with pepper and nutmeg. Most probably no salt will be needed because of the saltiness of the ham stock.

Serve very hot, garnished with a little fresh cream.

Tomato soup

Marquess of Exeter, Lyddington
chef: Mrs D. M. Lee

1 lb fresh tomatoes
2 oz ham
3 shallots
1 bayleaf
1 oz butter
1 pint chicken stock (page 171)
½ oz fine sago
2 lumps sugar
½ glass full-bodied brown sherry
double cream

Roughly chop the tomatoes, ham and shallots. Simmer the ham, bay leaf and shallots in the butter over a low flame, stirring. Add the tomatoes and cook slowly for 20 minutes. Sieve and return to the pan. Add the stock and bring to the boil. Add the sago and sugar and simmer for 5 minutes. Adjust the seasoning.

Serve the soup very hot, in hot plates, with the sherry in the centre, and the cream in a circle (poured over the back of a spoon) on top of the sherry.

Poulet au gratin à la crème landaise

Peacocks, Marlow
chef: Mrs Downing

1 fresh chicken about 3½ lb dressed
   weight, and its giblets
3 tablesp goose, duck or pork fat
4 large onions
¼ lb stewing beef
1 bunch parsley
2 oz unsmoked bacon
2 tablesp brandy
salt, pepper
½ clove garlic
¼ lb mushrooms
¼ pint double cream
1 teasp yellow French mustard
2 tablesp grated Parmesan

Joint the chicken, dividing it into
8 pieces, leaving the carcase to go
into the stock. Slice the onions finely
and fry them in 2 tablespoonsful of
fat. Add the beef, cut up, and the
giblets and brown them lightly. Add
the carcase. Pour 1¼ pints of water
over them, put in the bunch of
parsley and simmer it for an hour.
Strain it through a sieve and remove
any grease.

Melt another tablespoonful of fat in
a large saucepan or flameproof casserole, and brown the chicken joints
lightly. Remove them while frying
the diced bacon in the same fat.

Strain off the fat before putting the
chicken back. Pour the brandy over
it and set it alight. Season with salt
and pepper, then remove the pieces
of breast, which will take less time to
cook. Add the crushed garlic and
sliced mushrooms and pour the stock
over the chicken, letting it simmer
gently for 20 minutes. Put back the
breasts and continue to simmer for
another 15 minutes.

Transfer the chicken, bacon and
mushrooms to a warmed gratin dish
and keep hot. Take half a pint of the
stock the chicken was cooked in, put
it in a small saucepan and let it
reduce a little. Mix the cream and
mustard together and add them to
the stock. Let it bubble for a minute
or two before adding a tablespoonful
of the cheese. Stir until it has dissolved but do not let the sauce boil.

Check the seasoning, then pour the
sauce over the chicken. Sprinkle it
with more Parmesan and brown the
dish quickly under a hot grill.

Tarte aux pommes Joséphine (6)

Frederick's, London
chef: D. Jamard

for the shortcrust
6 oz sifted flour
3½ oz butter
1 egg
1 tablesp caster sugar
1 tablesp water

for the filling
1½ lb cooking apples
½ lb granulated sugar
2 tablesp water
apricot jam
2-3 peaches or some cherries

Line an 8-inch buttered flan case with the pastry and bake it blind (page 173). Cool it on a rack. Peel, core and slice the apples; put them in a bowl of cold water with a little lemon juice to prevent their going brown.

Put the sugar and water in a heavy saucepan over a low heat to caramelise. Shake the pan occasionally but do not stir. When the caramel is a rich golden colour, dry the apple slices and add them carefully to the pan. Cook them for about 5 minutes, or until they are soft but not pulped, turning them frequently with a wooden spoon. Leave them to cool.

Brush the flan case with some melted apricot jam. Spoon in the apples and a little of the caramel. Arrange the sliced peaches or cherries decoratively on top.

Reheat the remaining caramel and let it cook until it is darker in colour and rather syrupy. Pour it carefully over the tart and allow it to cool before serving.

95

Autumn menu 3

Inwoods savoury pancakes *or* **stuffed tomatoes**

ris de veau au beurre noisette, mashed potatoes, leeks in cream

Cold Love (6–8)

You may want to try this menu out on rather sophisticated friends, since all the dishes are unusual. As with liver, it is best to be sure that they will all enjoy sweetbreads. Not everyone does and it is a pity to make them suffer and waste the sweetbreads.

The savoury pancakes have a stuffing of cream cheese and spinach and a fresh tomato sauce. If you prefer a lighter first course, which requires no last-minute preparation, choose instead the tomatoes stuffed with tuna fish mayonnaise. Either is colourful and appetising. Ratatouille (page 54) would be a possible alternative.

The sweetbreads with their brown butter sauce are prepared in the classical way, blanched and simmered first and then either heated up in the beurre noisette or sliced and fried in butter with the beurre noisette as a sauce. The boiled leeks are finished with a little cream and breadcrumbs browned under the grill. Only mashed potatoes could counteract all this richness.

Cold Love will be very soothing after the first two courses, because it is a cold, lightly jellied custard flavoured with dark rum and containing mixed fresh fruit. However, if you prefer something lighter, an ordinary fresh fruit salad would be equally appropriate, as would apples or pears, with or without cheese.

Cold Love should be made the day before your party so that it can firm up in the refrigerator and be mellowed by the rum. Preparation of the sweetbreads can be started on the morning of the party, but their final sautéeing or heating in the beurre noisette must be done just before dinner. The pancakes are better if the batter stands for an hour or two. They can be made and stuffed shortly before dinner. The tomato sauce can also be made ahead, but the final marrying-up should be done at the last minute. The stuffed tomatoes can be prepared before the guests arrive; the leeks in cream should be finished at the same time as the sweetbreads.

Wine suggestions

<table>
<tr><td></td><td>MAIN COURSE</td><td>EITHER
claret (St Emilion, Pomerol)</td><td>OR
Rhine wine (Schloss Böckelheimer from the Nahe, Dürkheimer from the Palatinate)</td></tr>
</table>

Such a fine dish of sweetbreads calls for a good wine, whether red or white is your choice. From St Emilion, you could drink Ch. Figeac or Ch. Gaffelière-Naudes; from Pomerol, Ch. la Fleur-Pourret or Ch. l'Evangile. They should be at least seven years old. The hocks are full without being heavy; some develop a bouquet of honeysuckle.

Timetable

	DAY BEFORE	Cold Love – prepare and refrigerate overnight.
	ON THE DAY	
	morning	Soak sweetbreads for at least 2 hours.
	3 hours before dinner	Pancakes – make batter and leave to stand.
	2¼ hours before	Soak sweetbreads in water and vinegar for an hour. Pancakes – make tomato sauce.
	1¼ hours before	Sweetbreads – trim and simmer for 10 minutes. Make beurre noisette.
	1 hour before	Sweetbreads – leave to cool thoroughly, then dry. *either* – Pancakes – cook pancakes, prepare filling, stuff and keep hot. *or* – Stuffed tomatoes – prepare.
	¼ hour before	To serve sweetbreads sliced – dip slices in butter and sauté (do not add the beurre noisette). Put potatoes and leeks on to boil. Pre-heat oven to 375°F, mark 5.
	5 mins before	Pancakes – reheat tomato sauce.
	last minute	Leeks – complete preparation and put in oven. Whole sweetbreads – heat in beurre noisette and keep warm.
	between courses	Sliced sweetbreads – heat sweetbreads. Heat beurre noisette and pour it over. Mash potatoes.

Inwoods savoury pancakes

for the pancakes
½ pint batter (page 172)

for the sauce
1 onion
½ oz butter
1 tablesp oil
1½ lb tomatoes
1 teasp chopped parsley
  or celery leaves
1 clove garlic
2 basil leaves or ¼ teasp dried
  basil
1 teasp salt
1 teasp sugar
pepper

for the filling
1 lb spinach
½ lb cream cheese
salt, pepper
chopped parsley

Inwoods Restaurant, Five Ashes
chefs: Martin Harvey and Michael Carter

Make the pancake batter and allow it to stand for up to 2 hours.

Prepare the tomato sauce by chopping the onion and softening it in the heated butter and oil until it is transparent. Then add the skinned tomatoes, chopped roughly, the chopped herbs and the seasoning. Cover the saucepan and simmer for 20 minutes; rub the pulp through a sieve. Check the seasoning and keep the sauce warm while preparing the pancakes and filling or reheat it at the end.

While the sauce is simmering, wash and strip the spinach. Cook it without water for about 5 minutes until it is tender. Drain it very well, chop it

and season with salt and pepper before adding the cream cheese to it, and reheat gently.

Make 8 medium-sized pancakes and keep them hot. Put two spoonsful of the spinach filling in the centre of each pancake and roll it up. Arrange the pancakes on a heated serving dish and pour over the hot tomato sauce. Sprinkle with a little chopped parsley and serve immediately.

The pancakes could be made and stuffed a little beforehand and kept hot in a covered dish in the oven. But the sauce should be kept hot separately and poured over at the end.

Stuffed tomatoes

Old Priory Restaurant, Chichester
chef: Mrs Rzymkowski

4 large tomatoes
3½-oz tin salmon or tuna
½ pint thick mayonnaise (page 171)
salt, black pepper
chopped parsley
lettuce leaves

Cut a slice off the stalk end of each tomato. Scoop out the flesh without damaging their skins.

Drain and flake the fish, removing any skin or bones. Add to it the

mayonnaise and the salt and pepper. Fill the tomatoes with the fish mayonnaise, and sprinkle the tops with chopped parsley. Arrange the tomatoes on a serving dish and surround them with lettuce leaves.

Ris de veau au beurre noisette

L'Etoile, London
chef: Georges Ribiero

for the sweetbreads
1¼ lb calf's sweetbreads
water, vinegar, salt
¼ onion
small piece of carrot
½ bay leaf
1 clove
1 sprig thyme
4 peppercorns

for the sauce
3 tablesp wine vinegar, or lemon
   juice
6 oz clarified butter
   (page 168)
salt, pepper

for the final cooking
flour
1½ oz butter
1 tablesp cooking oil

for garnishing
2 tablesp finely chopped parsley

Soak the sweetbreads in several changes of cold water for 2 hours, and for a further hour in cold water with a teaspoonful of vinegar for each pint. Pull off as much of the membrane as possible without tearing the sweetbreads. Trim them by cutting the two lobes from the connecting tube.

Put the sweetbreads in a saucepan and cover them by two inches with cold water. Add salt (1 teaspoonful per quart), the onion, carrot, bayleaf, clove, thyme and peppercorns. Cook them, uncovered, just below simmering point, for about 10 minutes. Leave to cool in the stock, then dry them on absorbent paper.

Boil the wine vinegar briskly until it is reduced to a tablespoonful. Heat the clarified butter over a moderate heat until it turns brown; stir in the reduced vinegar and season with salt and pepper.

To serve the sweetbreads whole, add them to the butter and heat them through, basting periodically. To serve them sliced and sautéed, dip the slices lightly in flour. Melt the butter with a tablespoonful of oil over a moderate heat in a large frying pan. When the foam subsides, sauté the slices for 3 to 4 minutes on each side until they are lightly browned.

In either case, arrange them neatly on a heated serving dish. Reheat the brown butter and pour it over them. Sprinkle with chopped parsley and serve immediately.

Leeks in cream

Poacher's Inn, Piddletrenthide
chefs: Jill Fish and Ursula

4–6 leeks
4 fl oz single cream
salt, pepper
home-made, dried breadcrumbs
¾ oz butter

Cut the trimmed leeks in half lengthways, and boil them in salted water until they are just tender. Drain, and transfer them to a buttered ovenproof dish. Pour over the cream, sprinkle with a layer of breadcrumbs and dot with butter. Brown the top in a moderate oven (375°F, mark 5) or under the grill.

Cold Love (6-8)

Duke of York, Iddesleigh
chef: Joan Weekes
Mrs Rafferty, the proprietor, found this recipe in a Spanish cookery book.

a selection of fresh fruit
½ **small melon**
1 **pear**
¼ **lb strawberries**
½ **dessert apple**
¼ **lb grapes**
2–3 **plums**

2 **dessertsp sugar**
¼ **pint dark rum**
4 **egg yolks**
good pinch cinnamon
1 **pint milk**
¼ **lb vanilla sugar (page 169)**
1 **tablesp gelatine**
¼ **pint double cream**
single cream or whipped cream

Use whatever fruit is available, with as colourful a variety as possible.

Chop the melon, or make balls; peel and chop the pear and apple; halve the strawberries; halve the grapes and remove the pips (peel them only if the skins are tough); peel, stone and chop the plums. Sprinkle the fruit with sugar and soak it in the rum for 2–3 hours.

Make a custard in a heavy saucepan or double boiler with the egg yolks, cinnamon, milk and vanilla sugar.

Do not allow it to boil. Soften the gelatine in a tablespoonful of warm water. Stir it into the custard until it is completely dissolved.

Mix the fruit and custard and fold in the whipped cream. Chill for several hours. Serve with pouring cream.

EDITOR'S NOTE: the rum makes the custard an unusual beige colour. If you do not care for this, put a thin layer of single cream or piped whipped cream on top. The taste is delicious.

Autumn menu 4

chilled cream of mushroom soup *or* **potage de garbanzos**

roast duck with port and orange sauce *or* **pickled pineapple** *or* **prune and Beaujolais sauce, pureed potatoes and chestnuts, salad**

cherry and almond tart (6–8)

This is another meal which would be interesting for fellow cooks, since the dishes are the kind it is fun to talk about. The menu is flexible. On a cold day you could serve the hot Spanish soup, on a mild day the cold mushroom one.

The chilled cream of mushroom soup is rather lighter than the other and keeps the taste of raw mushrooms very well. It is a pinky-beige colour with flecks of fresh tarragon. The potage de garbanzos is an exotic blend of chick peas, spinach, almonds, garlic and onions, garnished with hard-boiled egg. It is a comforting soup, obviously more filling than the other.

The Howard Arms method of roasting a duck, and notes on other possible variations, are on page 162. One of three fruity sauces or pickles makes a change from the traditional sage-and-onion stuffing or apple sauce. Since all are sweet, it is worth experimenting until you find the actual degree of sweetness you prefer. The port and orange sauce also contains redcurrant jelly, and is sharpened by mustard and wine vinegar – a variation on Cumberland sauce, in fact. The pineapple is pickled with spices, vinegar and brown sugar. The prunes are cooked in Beaujolais until the mixture looks almost like a dark jam. With all this richness, try a green salad and the rather bland puree of potatoes and chestnuts (equal quantities of mashed potatoes and unsweetened chestnut puree, covered with buttered, toasted breadcrumbs and grated Cheddar, and baked in a moderate oven for about half an hour).

The cherry and almond tart uses tinned morello cherries in a creamy, almost curdlike filling based on ground almonds, which puffs up and browns as it cooks. The cherries sink into it, so that the result is a homely rather than an elegant sweet, with the sharpness of the cherries contrasting with the mildness of the filling. Oeufs à la neige (page 134) would make a suitable alternative, or apple and Stilton savoury (page 90).

All the preparation can be done beforehand except for the roasting of the duck, which must be timed to be ready just as you serve the first course. (We emphasise this after reading innumerable reports to the *Guide* complaining of dried-out ducks which restaurants have kept hot too long.)

Wine suggestions	MAIN COURSE	EITHER	OR
		Barolo, Nuits-St-Georges, or mature Beaujolais	Hock (Rheinhessen, eg. Niersteiner, Oppenheimer)

The sweet sauces with the duck will spoil many red wines; look for one that is full but not too dry. You could also try Fleurie or Morgon if you are having the prune-and-Beaujolais sauce. A dearer alternative – unconventional with duck, but none the worse for that – would be a fruity hock. Chill the hock. Open the Barolo 2–3 hours before dinner.

Timetable	A FEW DAYS BEFORE	Make pickled pineapple.
	THE DAY BEFORE	Make port and orange or prune and Beaujolais sauce.
		either Make mushroom soup and chill.
		or – Potage de garbanzos – soak chick peas.
	ON THE DAY	
	morning	Make cherry and almond tart.
	3 hours before dinner	Potage – start cooking chick peas.
	2 hours before	Mushroom soup – put into bowls and chill.
	1½ hours before	Pre-heat oven for duck.
	1¼ hours before	Start roasting duck.
	1 hour before	Put potatoes on to cook.
		Potage – finish soup and keep it hot.
	½ hour before	Complete preparation of potatoes and chestnuts, and put in the oven.
	¼ hour before	Duck – reheat sauce.
	5 mins before	Duck – remove to platter and keep warm.

Chilled cream of mushroom soup

Sharrow Bay Hotel, Ullswater
chef/proprietor: Francis Coulson

¼ lb white button mushrooms
7½ fl oz single cream
1 oz butter
1 oz flour
1 pint strong chicken stock
  (page 171)
salt, pepper
a little chopped fresh tarragon or
  parsley

Wipe the mushrooms with a damp cloth. Chop them roughly and either rub them through a sieve or blend them in a liquidiser with the cream.

Melt the butter in a 2-pint saucepan, blend in the flour and let it cook for a minute without browning, before gradually adding the stock. Bring gently to the boil, stirring continuously. Add the mushrooms and cream and simmer together for 5 minutes. Stir in some chopped tarragon or parsley, salt and pepper – add plenty, as a cold soup needs to be well seasoned.

Chill the soup for 2 or 3 hours. Serve with a little tarragon or parsley on top.

Potage de garbanzos

Simple Simon, London
chef: Señor Delgado

6 oz chick peas
½ teasp bicarbonate of soda
salt
1 medium-sized onion
2 tablesp olive oil
2 oz fresh spinach
½ teasp paprika
2 oz almonds
1 slice bread
3 large cloves of garlic
1 hard-boiled egg

Soak the chick peas overnight in plenty of water and the sodium bicarbonate.

Rinse them next day and put them into a pan with 2 pints of boiling, salted water. Bring it back to the boil and simmer gently until the peas are soft (from 1 to 4 hours.)

When they seem half cooked, chop the onion very finely and fry it in a tablespoonful of olive oil. Wash and strip the spinach and add it to the onion. Fry them for a few minutes, stir in the paprika and a little salt, and add this mixture to the chick peas. Cook until the peas are soft.

Fry the almonds in a tablespoonful of oil until they are golden. Drain and put them in a mortar. In the same oil, fry the diced bread until crisp and add it to the almonds. Peel the garlic and pound it to a paste with the almonds and bread. Stir this into the soup and continue to simmer for 10 minutes.

Check the seasoning; before serving, add the chopped hard-boiled egg.

EDITOR'S NOTE: some chick peas are specially treated so that they do not require soaking with bicarbonate of soda or prolonged cooking.

Pickled pineapple

Charlton House Hotel, Shepton Mallet
chef: Mrs Seaton

12-oz tin pineapple pieces
¼ lb brown sugar
1½ teasp pickling spice
7½ fl oz white vinegar

Drain the pineapple and put the pieces into a container – a glass screw-top jar, for example.

Mix the brown sugar, the juice and the spice in a pan and add the vinegar. Bring it slowly to the boil, stirring until the sugar is dissolved, and simmer for 15 minutes.

When the syrup has cooled a little, strain it and pour it over the pineapple. Cover when cold and keep for a few days before using it.

Port and orange sauce

Howard Arms, Ilmington
chef/proprietor: W. T. Last

½ lb redcurrant jelly
¼ pint port
1 teasp salt
freshly-ground black pepper
1 teasp dry mustard
2 teasp brown sugar
1 dessertsp wine vinegar
2 oranges
orange curaçao

Heat the jelly, port and seasonings to boiling point and simmer until the sauce is reduced to the desired thickness. Add the orange segments, each one cut in three, and a dash of curaçao. Reheat before serving.

EDITOR'S NOTE: the proportions for this sauce may be varied quite extensively. You may find, for example, that you prefer to use less port, so that the sauce does not need to be reduced, and so keeps some of its alcohol.

Prune and Beaujolais sauce

Howard Arms, Ilmington
chef/proprietor: W. T. Last

½ lb prunes
½ bottle Beaujolais
1 tablesp granulated sugar

Wash the prunes.

Bring the Beaujolais to the boil in a pan, stir in the sugar and add the prunes. Take the pan off the heat and leave the prunes to soak in the wine for 2 hours. Then reheat to simmering point, cover and cook for 1 to 1½ hours or until tender. Lift out the prunes with a slotted spoon, slit them open and remove the stones. Reduce the liquid a little and put the fruit back into it.

If the sauce has been prepared beforehand, reheat it just before dinner.

Cherry and almond tart

Box Tree Restaurant, Ilkley
chef/proprietors: Mr Reid and Mr Long

½ lb shortcrust pastry (page 173)
2 tablesp apricot jam
¼ lb unsalted butter
¼ lb caster sugar
2 eggs
¼ lb ground almonds
1 lb 14 oz tin of stoned, red morello cherries

Line a deep 9-inch flan case, buttered and floured, with the pastry. Prick the bottom lightly, then cover it with a coating of apricot jam. Preheat the oven to 375°F, mark 5, while preparing the filling. Beat the sugar into the softened butter until it is creamy. Beat in the eggs, one at a time, thoroughly. The mixture may separate, but this does not affect the final result. Mix in the ground almonds. Put the filling into the pastry case. Drain the cherries well, then arrange them on top of the filling. Bake on the middle shelf of the oven for 30–40 minutes until golden brown.

CHEF'S NOTE: the red, bitter morello cherries – called *griottes* in France – are an essential part of the dish.

EDITOR'S NOTES: since the filling puffs up in cooking, the container should be at least an inch deep.

The weight of the drained, stoned cherries should be just under 1 lb.

Autumn menu 5

Jaegermeister pâté with Waldorf salad

scampi façon Gourmet, with pilaff *or* **en brioche, lettuce salad**

chocolate cream with maraschino, *or* **crème velour**

This menu may sound both rich and expensive, but it is remarkably similar to what many people order in a restaurant. There is nothing unconventional here, but the dishes are particularly good. Once you have accepted it as a high-calorie meal, there is a balance of flavours and textures which prevents the richness from cloying.

The Jaegermeister pâté is a forceful one, with venison and liver as the basic ingredients, seasoned with mushrooms, herbs and brandy. The salad served with it is an agreeable contrast of crisp apples, celery and walnuts in mayonnaise. If you do not fancy venison – or do not have a liquidiser – you could use one of the other pâtés or terrines to be found in the index.

Instead of muffling the scampi in a coating of crumbs, this recipe prescribes a delicate cream sauce, flavoured with mushrooms and brandy, which complements their flavour perfectly. The sauce is mopped up either by rice pilaff (page 174) or by brioches (page 167) or by piped potato. A simple lettuce salad seems appropriate, since you will already have had the Waldorf salad with the pâté.

Both sweets are chocolate-mousse-like in appearance and texture, the first flavoured with maraschino and mellowed by its high butter-content, the second based on cream cheese with walnuts and brandy. If you cannot face so rich a meal, serve fresh fruit or spiced pears (page 47) instead.

The pâté is improved by being made the day before, so that the flavours can mingle. Either sweet could be made on the morning of the party, leaving you free to concentrate on the scampi at the last minute. If you wish to keep the dish hot while you eat the first course, use a bain-marie (page 168) so that the sauce will not curdle. You will still have to be in the kitchen for almost half an hour just before dinner, but you ought to be able to manage short appearances to talk to the guests and drink your aperitif.

Wine suggestions

MAIN COURSE

EITHER
white burgundy (Puligny-Montrachet, Meursault)

OR
Rüdesheimer, Swiss Chablais

An elegant wine, such as a fine burgundy, is needed to flatter the scampi and their creamy sauce. Choose a named vineyard (for example, Combettes for the Puligny, Genevrières for the Meursault). The hock from the Nahe or the Swiss wine are possible alternatives. Serve them lightly chilled. The first glass would go well with the pâté.

Timetable

THE DAY BEFORE

Make Jaegermeister pâté.
Brioche – make dough and put to rise. Combine dough with egg mixture and put to rise again. Tap down, cover, and prove overnight in the refrigerator.

ON THE DAY
morning

Make *either* chocolate cream with maraschino, and chill it *or* crème velour and chill it.

$1\frac{1}{2}$ hours before dinner

Prepare Waldorf salad.
Scampi – defrost if necessary.

$1\frac{1}{4}$ hours before
$\frac{1}{2}$ hour before

Brioche – knead and put to rise for about an hour.
Chop parsley.
Scampi – prepare ingredients and start cooking.
Brioche – pre-heat oven to 400°F, mark 6.

20 mins before
15 mins before
10 mins before
5 mins before

Brioche – put in oven.
Scampi – add béchamel and cream and simmer.
Cook pilaff.
Scampi – add cream and egg mixture. Cover and keep warm in a bain-marie.
Brioche – reduce oven heat to 350°F, mark 4.
Scoop out middle of brioche, butter and brown it in the oven.

between courses

either Brown scampi under grill
or Pour over the pilaff or into the brioche.
Sprinkle chopped parsley over scampi, or over pilaff if you are serving it.
Toss salad.

Jaegermeister pâté with Waldorf salad

½ lb shoulder of venison
¼ lb calf's liver
2 oz unsmoked bacon
1 medium-sized onion
1 oz margarine or lard
2 oz mushrooms
salt, pepper
about ¼ pint single cream
1 tablesp chopped parsley
1 small egg
good pinch of thyme or marjoram
1 tablesp brandy

Waldorf salad
4–6 eating apples
3 large sticks celery
6–8 walnuts
4 fl oz mayonnaise (page 171)

Central Hotel, Dover
chef/proprietor: Manfred Winands

Chop the venison, liver and bacon into fairly small pieces. Heat the fat in a large frying-pan and fry the venison quickly on all sides to seal it. Add the liver and bacon and fry briefly. Season with salt and pepper. Chop the onions and mushrooms and put them in a bowl with the meat. Stir in the chopped parsley, the beaten egg and about two-thirds of the cream. Blend this mixture in the liquidiser until it is smooth. If the mixture does not 'turn' easily at first, add more of the cream. Then stir in the herbs and the brandy and tip the mixture into a medium-sized terrine or pie dish.

Cover and bake in a bain-marie (page 168) in a moderate oven (350°F, mark 4) for 1½ hours. Remove the lid and continue to cook for a further 10 minutes to brown the top.

Let the pâté cool and leave it for 24 hours before eating.

Waldorf salad: peel and core the apples. Clean the celery. Chop the apples and walnuts coarsely, cut the celery into small thin slices, and fold them into the mayonnaise.

Scampi façon Gourmet

Restaurant du Gourmet, Bristol
chef/proprietor: Jean-Claude Denat

1½ lb large scampi
½ Spanish or French onion
1 oz butter
6 oz mushrooms
3 fl oz dry sherry
salt, pepper
¼ pint béchamel sauce (page 174)
8 fl oz double cream
1 egg yolk
parsley

If using frozen scampi, allow them to thaw. Chop the onion finely and cook it in the butter in a frying-pan until it is transparent. Add the scampi, the quartered or sliced mushrooms, the sherry, salt and pepper. Cook over a fairly high flame for a few minutes until slightly reduced.

Add the béchamel and all the cream except two spoonsful. Simmer gently for about 10 minutes. Mix the egg yolk with the rest of the cream and add it to the sauce, off the heat. Either brown the mixture quickly under the grill in a gratin dish or serve it on pilaff (page 174), en brioche (page 167), or in dishes or shells with piped potato round the edge. Decorate with parsley.

EDITOR'S NOTE: if you wish to serve this dish as a first course, use a pound of scampi and less sauce.

Chocolate cream with maraschino

Highbullen Country House Hotel, Chittlehamholt
chef: Mrs. Neil

2 oz plain chocolate, dessert or
   bitter
1 tablesp water
2 oz softened butter
½ oz caster sugar
2 eggs
1 tablesp maraschino liqueur

Break the chocolate into small pieces. Put it to melt with the water on a very low heat.

Cream the butter and the sugar. Separate the eggs and add the yolks one at a time, beating them in thoroughly. Add the melted chocolate and the liqueur.

Whisk the egg whites until they are very stiff, and fold them in gently. Put into individual chocolate pots or ramekins, and chill in the refrigerator for about 2 hours.

EDITOR'S NOTE: as chocolate overheats easily, use a *small* heavy saucepan, preferably a non-stick one, or a double boiler.

Crème velour

Jasper's, London
chef: F. Garcia

6 oz Philadelphia cream cheese
1½ oz caster sugar
2 large eggs
½ pint double cream
2½ oz good dessert chocolate,
   e.g. Chocolat-Menier
1 oz crushed walnuts
2 tablesp brandy or sherry

Beat the sugar into the cream cheese until it is smooth. Separate the eggs and beat in the yolks, one at a time, until the mixture is creamy. Whip the cream until it is fairly stiff and, continuing to whip, blend in the cream cheese mixture.

Melt the chocolate as described above. Stir it into the cheese mixture with the crushed walnuts and the brandy or sherry. Whip the egg whites until they are very stiff, and fold them in also.

Pour the *crème* into a glass bowl or into individual dishes and chill in the refrigerator for 2–3 hours. It can either be served plain, or decorated with whole or chopped walnuts or chocolate flakes; and as it is a light mousse, some kind of biscuit or wafer would go well with it.

Autumn menu 6

cream of cauliflower soup (6) *or* **scallop and artichoke soup**

pork Basil Brush, rösti, courgettes

hot fruit salad *or* **peach Melba**

Try this meal at a family party including children. It is not very expensive, the dishes are not so elaborate that most children will refuse to try them, the recipes can easily be expanded, and the name of Basil Brush should help the main course to go down well.

Both soups are creamy to look at. The scallop and artichoke one is enlivened by the bright pink corals. If you want the simpler taste, choose the cauliflower soup; if you think it's time to encourage even the children towards adult pleasures, serve the scallop and artichoke. You could always try the fresh tomato (page 93) – probably a new experience for the children.

Pork Basil Brush has cubed fillet cooked with stock, port and herbs, to produce a rich brown sauce. The meat is tender, lean, and easy for even the very young to eat. The crisp, golden potato cake goes well with it and if peas are top favourite this week, they could be substituted for the courgettes.

Hot fruit salad – with its rum and sugar-glazed cream topping – might seem more appropriate to an adult party, but if you would like to serve it to children without the rum, you could do so. Be sure that you get the right bowl!
On the other hand, peach Melba can offend no one and may seem a safer choice. It calls for a good ice-cream, preferably home-made, fresh peaches and a sauce made with fresh raspberries. It will almost certainly be totally unlike the version you have suffered in some restaurants.

The stocks for the soups and the pork can be made the day before the party, so that the soups themselves take relatively little time on the actual day. Pork Basil Brush can be prepared well ahead, as can the fruit for hot fruit salad. The last-minute jobs, which can be spaced round pauses for chat, include finishing the soups and the pork dish and cooking the rösti. If you are brave and competent, invite the children into the kitchen and toss the potato cake in traditional Swiss fashion.

Wine suggestions

<table>
<tr><td>MAIN COURSE</td><td>EITHER</td><td>OR</td></tr>
</table>

MAIN COURSE

EITHER
mature Beaujolais
(Moulin-à-Vent, Morgon)
Moulin-à-Vent and Morgon are the weightiest
of the Beaujolais wines, and are usually better for a
few years in bottle (1967 and 1969 are the best
recent vintages). The best Valpolicellas are dry,
light and fragrant – it is worth tracking down a
good one, bottled by a small house. It should not
be too expensive.

OR
Valpolicella

Timetable

THE DAY BEFORE	For either soup – make chicken stock.
	For the pork – make a meat stock.
ON THE DAY	
morning	*either* Make cauliflower soup
	or Start scallop and artichoke soup (do not add the scallops).
3 hours before dinner	Hot fruit salad – prepare the fruit salad.
	Peach Melba – cook peaches and make sauce.
1¾ hours before	Prepare and brown pork fillets.
1½ hours before	Pre-heat oven to 275°F, mark 1.
1¼ hours before	Pork – put fillets in a casserole into the oven.
	Prepare rösti.
25 mins before	Start cooking rösti.
	Hot fruit salad or peach Melba – whip the cream.
¼ hour before	Cauliflower soup – reheat and garnish.
	Scallop and artichoke soup – poach scallops and finish soup.
10 mins before	Cook courgettes and keep them warm.
after main course	Peach Melba – fill glasses.
	Hot fruit salad – complete the preparation and glaze.

Cream of cauliflower soup (6)

The Lands of Loyal Hotel, Alyth
chef/proprietors: Mr & Mrs Gavin Billinghurst

1 medium-sized cauliflower
2 small onions
4 small potatoes
1 oz ham or rind
bouquet garni (page 168)
1½ pints chicken stock (page 171)
salt, pepper
2 oz butter
2 oz flour
½ pint milk
cream

Wash the cauliflower and break it into sprigs. Peel the onions and potatoes and chop them up. Put the vegetables into a pan with the ham, the bouquet garni and the chicken stock. Add some salt and pepper if the stock is not already seasoned. Bring gently to the boil, then simmer. As soon as the cauliflower is tender but not overcooked, lift out some of the sprigs and keep them for garnishing. Continue simmering the soup until all the vegetables are cooked.

Remove the bouquet garni. Put the soup through a liquidiser, a vegetable mill, or a sieve.

Melt the butter in a separate pan, blend in the flour and gradually stir in the milk. Add this sauce to the soup, bring it to the boil and simmer for another 5 minutes. Just before serving, garnish the soup with the cooked sprigs of cauliflower and a swirl of cream.

Scallop and artichoke soup

Lacy's, London
chef: Bill Lacy

1 Spanish onion
1 oz butter
¾ lb Jerusalem artichokes
1 medium-sized potato
1 pint well-seasoned chicken
   stock (page 171)
salt, pepper
2 large or 3 small scallops
¼ pint milk
1 egg yolk
3 tablesp cream
chopped parsley

Cook the chopped onion in butter until soft and transparent. Add the peeled and sliced Jerusalem artichokes and potato. Stir until they are all buttery. Cook gently for about 15 minutes. Add the chicken stock, cover and simmer for about 20 minutes longer. Then put through a liquidiser, a vegetable mill or a sieve. Return to the pan and season with salt and pepper.

Poach the white part of the scallops lightly in the milk, cut them into dice and add them, along with the milk in which they were cooked, to the soup. Heat it gently, stir in the egg yolk beaten up with the cream and let the soup thicken without boiling. Just before serving add the uncooked scallop corals cut into 2 or 3 pieces, and scatter really lavishly with chopped parsley.

Pork Basil Brush

Manor House, Gaunts Earthcott
The St John-Brooks's have Basil Brush's permission to name this dish after him –
and a paw-marked certificate to prove it

1¼ lb pork fillet
1 small onion
4 tablesp olive oil
¼ teasp dried basil
¼ teasp dried sage
⅛ teasp powdered dill
6 tablesp tawny port
3 tablesp flour
1 pint meat stock, preferably
   ½ pint ham, ½ pint beef (page 170)
salt, pepper

Trim the pork fillet of any fat and cut it into ½-inch slices. Chop the onion. Heat the oil in a large frying-pan, and sweat the onion briefly before adding the herbs and 2 table-spoonsful of the port. Cook until the onion is transparent. Transfer it to an ovenproof casserole to keep warm. In the remaining fat in the pan, lightly brown the pork slices on all sides. Add these to the casserole. Stir the flour into the pan juices, then slowly add the stock and two more tablespoonsful of port. Stir until the sauce boils and has thickened slightly, season if necessary, and pour it over the pork in the casserole. Cover and cook in a slow oven (275°F, mark 1) for 1½ hours.

Five minutes before serving, stir in two more tablespoonsful of port.

EDITOR'S NOTE: ham stock is usually so salty that it would be wise to use it with unseasoned beef stock.

Rösti

The Old Manor House, Knaresborough
Rösti vies with fondue as the Swiss national dish. This version comes from the
Swiss chef/proprietor, Mr Schwaller, who also recommends it for breakfast with eggs

1 lb potatoes
1 large onion
salt, pepper
2 oz butter
1 tablesp oil

Boil the potatoes in their jackets. Stop cooking when they are still firm. Cool them slightly, peel and grate them coarsely. Chop the onion finely and mix it with the potato and salt and pepper.

Heat the butter and oil in an 8-inch frying-pan. When the fat is really hot, put in the potato mixture and press it down with a spatula so that the bottom of the pan is completely covered with a firm layer. Turn down the heat and leave to brown on the underside without disturbing it, for 10 to 15 minutes.

The rösti has then to be turned over, either by tossing or by inverting the pan onto a large plate and sliding the potato cake back into it. Continue the cooking for a further 10 minutes to brown the other side.

Hot fruit salad

Lacy's, London
chef: Bill Lacy

a selection of fresh fruit
raspberries
strawberries
peaches
pears
melon
oranges
grapes

Jamaican rum
¼ pint double cream
soft brown sugar

Using whatever fresh fruit is available and as colourful a medley as possible, make a fruit salad in the usual way. Prepare it some time beforehand and it will make its own juices (if there does not seem sufficient, add a little fresh orange juice).

Just before serving, spoon it into individual, flameproof dishes. Sprinkle it with the rum, and cover with a cloud of softly whipped cream. Over this scatter, quite thickly but randomly so that not all the surface is covered by it, pale sandy brown sugar.

Put the bowls under a *very* hot pre-heated grill. Watch carefully for the sugar to darken and sink into the cream and the surface to begin to blister – but don't let it get too black.

EDITOR'S NOTE: a high proportion of naturally sweet fruit will give the salad the right degree of sweetness. Otherwise you may need to add a little sugar syrup. Remove the membranes as well as the pith and seeds from the orange segments.

Peach Melba

Halland Motel and Old Forge Restaurant, Halland
chef: Salvatore Marrone

4 fresh peaches
¾ lb caster sugar
a vanilla pod
1 pint water
½ lb fresh raspberries
vanilla ice-cream
¼ pint double cream
4–8 perfect raspberries

Peel, halve and stone the peaches. Simmer together the ½ lb of sugar and the vanilla pod in the water until the sugar has dissolved.

Put the peaches into it and continue to simmer for 10–12 minutes. Leave them to cool in the syrup. When they are cold, drain them.

Rub the raspberries through a sieve and then beat or liquidise them with the remaining sugar until it has dissolved and the sauce is thick.

Half fill each glass with vanilla ice-cream. Arrange the peach halves on top. Pour some of the raspberry sauce over and top with sweetened, whipped cream. For a decoration, put one or two whole raspberries on top.

sole Baie des Anges, salad

apricot streusel

This menu – in expanded quantities – would make a very pleasant buffet supper, to be served after a cocktail party or other function where something tasty and sobering is required, without too much strain being put on the cook. Pancakes and cheese sauce make an ideal blotter for alcohol; the sweet is both large and handsome enough to give a sense of occasion. If you enjoy the cocktail party so much that you invite back more people than you have tables and chairs for, the whole meal can be eaten standing, fork in hand.

Sole Baie des Anges consists of lemon sole, mussels and mushrooms wrapped in pancakes, covered with cheese sauce and baked in the oven. Although the recipe suggests that you cook and serve the fish in individual gratin dishes, you would be wiser to use a larger dish if you plan a large buffet party, so that people can help themselves to a pancake onto a plate which will not burn their fingers. Almost any mixed or green salad would go well with the pancakes, but the dressing should be a light vinaigrette rather than a creamy one, since you already have a rich sauce with the pancakes. Apricot streusel may be familiar from afternoon teas in Germany or Austria. A sweetened pastry base is covered with a layer of apricots, topped with cinnamon-flavoured crumbs and served, of course, with plenty of cream.

All the preparation except for the final cooking of the pancakes in their sauce could be done ahead of time, so that you have only the pancakes to heat and the salad to toss at the last minute.

Wine suggestions

MAIN COURSE

EITHER
champagne

OR
white Loire (Anjou, Sancerre)

Champagne revives both mind and body, and is hard to resist for a late party. Every brand has its own style and advocates, so choose one you like and can afford. The driest are called 'brut'.
Savennières (from Anjou) and Sancerre are both dry; the lightness of the Sancerre makes it very appropriate for a late supper.
Serve all of these wines chilled.

DESSERT

EITHER
champagne

OR
Coteaux du Layon or Monbazillac

Continue with the champagne – perhaps a rich one this time – or have a glass of the sweet Anjou or Dordogne wines – less usual and less expensive choices than a Graves or Sauternes.

Sole Baie des Anges

Trewince, Port Navas
chef: Mrs Myers
This dish is named after Baie des Anges in Brittany, which Mr and Mrs Myers often visit.

½ pint batter (page 172)

for the fish stock
1 lb (approx) fish, bones or
   trimmings
1 small onion
6 parsley stalks
1 teasp lemon juice
¼ teasp salt
¼ pint dry white wine

for the filling
1 lemon sole in 4 fillets
¼ pint dry white wine
24 mussels
¼ lb mushrooms
½ oz butter
salt, pepper
juice of half a lemon

for the sauce
2 oz butter
2 oz flour
2 tablesp double cream (optional)
2 oz grated cheese

Make the pancake batter (page 172) and allow it to stand for at least 2 hours.

Prepare the fish stock by simmering the ingredients in an open pan, with enough water to cover them, for half an hour. Skim when necessary. Strain the stock and correct the seasoning.

Make 4 large pancakes.

Season the fillets and partly cook them in the wine for 10 minutes in a moderate oven (350°F, mark 4).

Reserve the wine. Clean the mussels (page 122); remove them from their shells by heating them in a large saucepan for a few minutes in a little of the fish stock. Strain their liquor back into the stock. Slice the mushrooms and sauté them quickly for a few minutes in butter.

Place one fillet in the centre of each pancake, cover with some of the mussels and mushrooms. Season with salt, pepper and a little lemon juice. Fold over the sides of each pancake to make a parcel, and put into four buttered gratin dishes.

Make a roux (page 169) with the butter and flour. Stir in three quarters of a pint of fish stock and the wine the fish was poached in. Bring to the boil, stirring continuously and add the cream, and some of the grated cheese.

Pour the sauce over the pancakes, sprinkle with the rest of the cheese and bake in a moderate oven (350°F, mark 4) until golden – about 20 minutes.

Apricot streusel

Grange Hotel, Grange-in-Borrowdale
chef: Mrs Arnesen

½ lb sweet shortcrust pastry
(page 173)
2–3 tablesp apricot jam
¾ lb fresh, stoned apricots or
1 large tin
5 oz sifted flour
1 oz ground almonds
3 oz butter
2 oz caster sugar
cinnamon
sugar
cream

Make the pastry; let it rest in a cool place or the refrigerator. Roll out a circle to fit the base of a 7-inch flan ring. Butter and flour the ring, and lay in the pastry. Prick it and spread warmed apricot jam over it.

Halve the fresh apricots or drain the tinned ones thoroughly. Put 3 or 4 of the firmest halves on one side for decorating, and arrange half of the remaining ones on top of the jam. If fresh ones are being used, sprinkle a little sugar over them at this point.

Make the streusel by mixing the flour and ground almonds, then rubbing the butter into the mixture until it is like fine breadcrumbs; stir in the sugar. Cover the apricots with a layer of this mixture. Arrange the remaining half quantity of apricots on top, then cover the whole with the rest of the streusel, firming it slightly with the fingertips.

Bake in a fairly hot oven (400°F, mark 6) for about 15 minutes, then reduce the heat to 325°F, mark 3, for another 20–30 minutes until the top is golden and firm. When cool, sprinkle with caster sugar to which a small pinch of cinnamon has been added. Decorate with the firm apricots cut into slices. Serve cold with plenty of cream.

CHEF'S NOTE: rhubarb with ginger, or apple with lemon, make good alternatives to apricots.

Winter menu 1

moules marinière *or* **mussels in cream and curry sauce**

casseroled pheasant, puree of swedes and carrots

oranges in chocolate *or* **naranjas al kirsch**

You will want a special occasion and perhaps special people to enjoy this meal, which is caviare to the general. Seasonal mussels and pheasant, both rich dishes, are contrasted with the fresh oranges of the last course.

Whichever recipe you choose for mussels, you follow the same method initially, cooking the cleaned mussels in wine flavoured with herbs and shallots. The moules marinière are finished with cream and served in their shells. (Provide a fork for scooping them out, a soup spoon for the fragrant broth, a dish for the empty shells, and a finger bowl for cleaning up.) For the other dish, the mussels are removed from the shells and served in individual ramekins with a gentle, creamy curried sauce. If mussels cannot be had, you could start with a small helping of scampi façon Gourmet (page 108) or a pâté or terrine.

The casseroled pheasant is similar to faisan à l'alsacienne (in which pheasant is served with sauerkraut), except that this recipe has fresh cabbage, spiced with Polish sausage, bacon and onions. After the long, slow cooking in wine, the cabbage becomes dark brown and you may prefer to serve a green vegetable or salad with it rather than the suggested puree of swedes and carrots (rather more carrot than swede, with butter, salt, pepper and nutmeg).

If you think that your guests can take still more calories and a raised cholesterol level, serve the orange segments coated with dessert chocolate, and decorated with whipped cream and Cointreau. But it will do no harm to choose the simpler orange slices with kirsch, which are as easy to prepare as to eat.

The casseroled pheasant and the oranges in chocolate should be started well ahead of dinner time. The mussels need a little last-minute attention but this is by no means a hectic meal to prepare. If you don't want your house to smell of swedes, prepare the puree ahead and heat it, covered for the first 20 minutes or so, in the oven with the pheasant for about half an hour.

Wine suggestions

APERITIF AND FIRST COURSE	EITHER	OR
	Sancerre	Muscadet

Both the Sancerre from the upper Loire and the Muscadet from around Nantes are light, dry and fresh. Muscadet, which is cheaper, can be acid, so choose carefully. Both should be drunk young, and chilled.

MAIN COURSE	EITHER	OR
	Rhône (Côte Rôtie)	Pilsner lager

A robust wine is needed to stand up to the highly-seasoned pheasant casserole. A Rhône, such as Côte Rôtie, or a Châteauneuf-du-Pape could do it, but you may prefer to serve a well-chilled Pilsner. (Remember that some people do not like drinking wine and beer during the same meal.)

Timetable

ON THE DAY

morning	Oranges in chocolate – prepare and chill.
	Moules marinière – scrub mussels.
	Mussels in cream and curry sauce – Scrub the mussels and steam them open. Reserve the liquor. When mussels are cool remove them from their shells.
3 hours before dinner	Pheasant – prepare and start cooking.
1 hour before	Naranjas al kirsch – prepare.
$\frac{3}{4}$ hour before	Cook vegetables.
$\frac{1}{2}$ hour before	Mussels in cream and curry – prepare.
$\frac{1}{4}$ hour before	Moules marinière – prepare.
	Mussels in cream – put in oven.

Moules marinière

Au Bon Accueil, London
chef: Ronald Pearce

2 quarts mussels
2 oz butter
4 shallots
2 tablesp chopped parsley
freshly ground black pepper
6 fl oz dry white wine
4 fl oz double cream

Keep the mussels alive in water until it is time to prepare them. Scrub each mussel thoroughly under cold running water. Scrape off any barnacles and pull off the 'beard'. Make sure all the sand is cleaned off, and discard any mussels already open or whose shells are loose.

Melt the butter in a large saucepan. Put the finely chopped shallots into the pan with the chopped parsley and the pepper. When they have softened in the butter on a low flame, add the mussels and the white wine. Cover the pan and turn up the heat, shaking the pan from time to time and turning the mussels over. When all are open, take them out of the pan and put them into a large soup tureen or individual bowls.

Pour the cream into the pan of liquor, bring it to the boil and then pour it over the mussels. In case there is still a little sand in the the sauce, do not use the last spoonful.

Mussels in cream and curry sauce

The Garden, London
chef: Enzo di Battista

for the mussels
2 quarts mussels
2 oz butter
3–4 shallots or 1 onion
few sprigs parsley
1 bay leaf
3 fl oz dry white wine
3 fl oz water

for the sauce
1 oz butter
½ oz flour
½ oz curry powder
¼ pint double cream

Prepare the mussels as described above, and steam them open in the same way with the butter, shallots, herbs, wine and water. When all have opened, the mussels must be removed from their shells; let them cool a little and pull each one away carefully. Divide them among four small dishes and save the liquor.

Make a roux (page 169) with the butter, flour and curry powder. Let it cook a little, then blend in enough of the strained stock from the mussels to make a sauce that is not too thick. Add the cream and simmer for a few minutes before pouring it over the mussels.

Put the ramekins into a fairly hot oven (400°F, mark 6) for 5–10 minutes* – to reheat, but not to cook further.

EDITOR'S NOTE: *15 minutes at 325°F, mark 3, if you are cooking the pheasant at the same time.

Casseroled pheasant

*Brooklands Restaurant, Dodworth
chef: Larry*

1 large or 2 small pheasants
6 oz unsmoked bacon
2 shallots or 2 cloves of garlic
½ teasp crushed rosemary leaves
2 oz butter
3 fresh Polish pork sausages
2 tablesp bacon or pork fat
½ hard, white cabbage, (about 1 lb)
salt, pepper
¼ pint dry white wine
white wine vinegar (optional)

Wipe the inside of the bird and fill it with a stuffing made from 4 ounces of the bacon, the shallots or garlic and the rosemary, all chopped together. Melt the butter in a frying-pan and brown the pheasant all over, also the sausages, cut into inch lengths.

While the bird is browning, melt the bacon fat in a flameproof casserole. Discard the hard stalk and slice the cabbage finely across so that it is like spaghetti. Fry it in the bacon fat until it is fairly soft but not completely cooked. Season.

Put the pheasant on top of the cabbage and cover it with the remaining slices of bacon. Arrange the sausages round the bird and pour the wine over it. If the wine is not a very dry one, add a little vinegar.

Cover and cook in a fairly slow oven (325°F, mark 3) until the pheasant is tender – 1 hour to 1¾ hours, depending upon the age and size of the bird.

CHEF'S NOTE: if Polish sausage is not available, a good Cumberland sausage or Bratwurst will do.

Oranges in chocolate

The Priory, Bath
chef/proprietor: Thea Dupays

4 large oranges
½ lb plain chocolate (preferably a
    good quality bitter chocolate)
1 tablesp water
Cointreau
¼ pint double cream

Cut off the peel and the white pith of the oranges with a sharp knife; cut out the segments without their skins. Pat them dry with a teacloth or absorbent paper to remove any excess juice. Cover two baking trays with sheets of oiled grease-proof paper.

Break the chocolate into small pieces. Put it to melt with a tablespoonful of water on a very low heat, either in a small pan or preferably a double-boiler as chocolate burns easily.

Drop the segments one at a time into the chocolate, turn them over to coat both sides and remove them with tongs to the oiled paper. Put the trays in the refrigerator or a very cool place for a few hours to set.

Arrange the slices on a dish and sprinkle them liberally with Cointreau. Serve with whipped cream.

EDITOR'S NOTE: alternatively, the Cointreau could be folded into the whipped cream.

Naranjas al kirsch

Andalucia Restaurant, Rugby
chef: Carlos Garcia Gamblor

3 large or 4 medium-sized oranges
kirsch

Cut off the peel from the oranges with a sharp knife as closely as possible to the flesh so that no white pith is left on the fruit. Then slice each orange into 6 or 8 slices.

Arrange the slices overlapping in a shallow dish, and pour over them about 4 tablespoonsful of kirsch – use enough so that the fruit will have a sharp tang.

If this dish is prepared some time in advance, the orange slices absorb the liqueur well but lose some of their refreshing, juicy texture, and the juice may need a final further dash of kirsch to sharpen it again.

Winter menu 2

mushrooms in garlic butter *or* **orange and celery salad with hot garlic bread**

coddled pockets, spinach, egg noodles

parfait au marron (6) *or* **flummery Drambuie**

The combination of highly-coloured and highly-seasoned dishes in this menu makes one think of youth and enthusiasm rather than age and sophistication. There is a mixture of new flavours and new methods to encourage experiments, in honour perhaps of a birthday or some other celebration where formality is less important than fun.

The mushrooms in the first recipe are grilled under a pat of the garlic butter more commonly used with snails. The flavour is just as good as it is with snails and there is no juggling with tongs. If you prefer to serve a salad, the orange and celery one, with a herby vinaigrette, would go well with hot garlic bread (page 165). But if you prefer to play down the garlic, you could serve smoked trout pâté (page 40) or fresh herring pâté (page 160).

Coddled pockets, in spite of its old English name, looks very Italian on the plate. Veal escalopes are rolled round forcemeat and served with two sauces, one cheese, the other tomato. The completed dish is glazed under the grill and would look handsome with noodles and spinach to accentuate the colours and the Italian flavours. However, if you have not served salad as first course, a green salad would go just as well.

Parfait au marron is a mousse of chestnut puree and chocolate; flummery Drambuie is rather like zabaglione with liqueur instead of Marsala. If you prefer to have a sweet without cream, you could serve instead either naranjas al kirsch (page 124) or a fresh fruit salad.

The marron parfait should be made the day before it is to be eaten, and the garlic butter also improves with chilling. Flummery Drambuie should be made on the morning of the party, and the first preparations for the coddled pockets can also be carried out then. Garlic bread too, can be prepared several hours ahead. You will then be left to finish the mushrooms and the coddled pockets, and to prepare the salad in the hour or so before the party.

Wine suggestions

<table>
<tr><td></td><td>MAIN COURSE</td><td>EITHER
Italian (Bardolino, Chianti, Grignolino)</td><td>OR
Australian red (Coona-warra) or inexpensive claret (Côte de Bourg, Fronsac)</td></tr>
</table>

Coddled pockets is so Italian in concept that an Italian wine seems an appropriate choice. The three we name vary considerably in character. The garlicky first course makes subtle appreciation of wine difficult and if you do choose a claret, a minor one would be perfectly adequate. There are several sound Australian wines of the same type, made from the cabernet grape.

Timetable

THE DAY BEFORE

Parfait au marron – prepare and chill overnight.
Mushrooms or garlic bread – prepare and chill garlic butter.

ON THE DAY
morning

Flummery Drambuie – prepare and chill.
Coddled pockets – prepare stuffing, fill escalopes and roll them up.
Prepare tomato sauce.
Garlic bread – prepare.

$1\frac{1}{4}$ hours before dinner

Orange and celery salad – prepare but do not toss in dressing.

1 hour before

Fry mushrooms.
Decorate either sweet.

$\frac{3}{4}$ hour before

Coddled pockets – start cooking; make cream sauce.
Heat tomato sauce.

$\frac{1}{2}$ hour before

Pre-heat oven to 400°F, mark 6.

$\frac{1}{4}$ hour before

Put garlic bread in oven.
Fry coddled pockets.

10 mins before

Mushrooms – complete the preparation.

last minute

Coddled pockets – reduce oven heat to 375°F, mark 5, and put pockets in.
Orange and celery salad – toss in dressing.

between courses

Complete and glaze coddled pockets.

Mushrooms in garlic butter

Thornbury Castle, Thornbury
chef/proprietor: Kenneth Bell

6 oz Normandy butter
2 small cloves garlic
¾ level teasp salt
¾ oz onion
1 small lemon
5 turns of pepper mill
nutmeg
chopped parsley
2 oz fresh breadcrumbs
1 lb button mushrooms
2 oz clarified butter (page 168)

Put the six ounces of butter in a heavy bowl and cream it with a wooden spoon. Add the garlic crushed with the salt, the finely chopped onion, the lemon rind and juice, the pepper, nutmeg, parsley and breadcrumbs. Form the mixture into a cylinder, wrap it and chill it in the refrigerator.

Wash and dry the mushrooms and fry them in the clarified butter over fairly high heat until half cooked. Lift them out and put them on one side.

Just before dinner, divide the mushrooms among four small, fireproof dishes (or put them in a gratin dish), cover with slices of the garlic butter and put under a very hot grill until brown on top. Serve immediately, with some French bread to mop up the butter.

CHEF'S NOTES: you will need less salt if using salted butter.
If there is any garlic butter left over, it can be used on steaks or other grills. It can also be used with snails.

Orange and celery salad

Poacher's Inn, Piddletrenthide
chefs: Jill Fish and Ursula

3–4 oranges
1 small head of celery
vinaigrette (page 172)
herbs
garlic

Peel the oranges and remove all the pith. Divide them into segments and cut each segment into three. Clean the celery and select the best pieces from the heart – about 6–8 sticks, to make an equal quantity with the orange.

Chop the celery into fairly small pieces, mix it with the pieces of orange and toss the salad in a vinaigrette which has been well seasoned with herbs and garlic.

Coddled pockets

The Bell Inn, Ramsbury
Brian O'Malley creates his recipes from ideas found in Hannah Glasse, The Complete Housewife, and other books; he uses the old names but updates the methods.

8 small escalopes of veal
2 oz veal – scraps or stewing veal
2 oz cooked ham
6 oz pork sausage meat
salt, pepper, ground mace
1 clove garlic
1 egg yolk
2 tablesp flour
1 oz butter

for the tomato sauce
1 medium-sized onion
½ oz butter
1-lb tin Italian plum tomatoes
2 cloves garlic
salt, pepper

for the cream sauce
1 teasp arrowroot
½ teasp turmeric
¼ pint cream
2 oz Cheddar

for the glaze
Parmesan

The veal escalopes should be long, narrow ones. Beat them out flat under polythene or waxed paper, using a rolling pin or meat bat.

Make the forcemeat by pounding in a mortar or mincing finely together the scraps of veal, the ham and the sausage meat. Season with a crushed clove of garlic, salt, pepper and mace. Form this forcemeat into eight sausages and roll up each one in an escalope. Tie them round with cotton or fine string. Dip them in beaten egg yolk, then the flour, and fry in an ounce of butter for about 15 minutes, turning them until the 'pockets' are golden all over.

Transfer to an earthenware or ovenproof dish and continue cooking for 10 minutes in a moder-ately hot oven (375°F, mark 5). Remove the strings.

To make the tomato sauce, chop the onion finely and cook it gently in half an ounce of butter until it is soft and transparent. Add the chopped tomatoes, 2 crushed cloves of garlic, salt and pepper, and cook until most of the moisture has evaporated.

To make the cream sauce, blend the arrowroot and the turmeric with the cream, mix in the grated Cheddar and heat slowly, stirring continuously until it is creamy and smooth.

Pour the tomato sauce over the 'pockets', then the cream sauce, sprinkle with a little grated Parmesan and brown quickly under a hot grill.

Parfait au marron (6)

Yew Tree Inn, Odstock
chef: Mrs Gould

¼ lb bitter cooking chocolate
3 oz caster sugar
2½ fl oz water
1 lb tin unsweetened chestnut
  puree
2 eggs
6 oz softened butter
whipped cream
chocolate vermicelli

Break the chocolate into pieces, put it in a saucepan with the sugar and water, and stir it over a gentle heat until the chocolate and sugar have melted. Leave it to cool slightly, then mix it into the chestnut puree.

Separate the eggs and beat the yolks into the mixture, one at a time. Cut the butter into pieces, and beat them in – an electric mixer makes this stage a much easier one. Whisk the egg whites until they are stiff, then fold them into the mixture.

Butter a 1¾-pint mould, or two small ones and fill with the mixture. Cover and place in the refrigerator until the following day.

Turn the parfait out of its mould and serve it with whipped cream, decorated with chocolate vermicelli.

Flummery Drambuie

Open Arms Hotel, Dirleton
chef: H. Johnstone

4 egg yolks
3 tablesp caster sugar
3 tablesp Drambuie
7½ fl oz double cream

Put the egg yolks and sugar into a double boiler, or a basin which will fit over a saucepan of simmering water. Using a rotary beater or a balloon whisk, whip together quickly the eggs and sugar. When the mixture thickens and has increased in volume, add the Drambuie. Continue beating until the mixture is stiff and will stand in peaks. Whip the cream until it is semi-stiff and fold it in gently.

Pour the flummery into saucer-shaped champagne glasses or shallow glass dishes and chill. Before serving, the top of each can be decorated with a piped rosette of whipped cream.

Winter menu 3

coquilles St Jacques, Hotel de la Poste

carbonnade flamande, parsley potatoes

oeufs à la neige

This is a French menu, but not one you would be likely to find in France, since the first course is haute cuisine, the second peasant cooking and the last straight from the nursery. But it makes an agreeable meal for francophiles or tyros about to travel. If you vary the first and last courses, try to keep to French dishes (see the index under *French*) so that the sketchy homogeneity is sustained. The first and last courses require some patience and skill; both are highly rewarding.

The coquilles St Jacques from the Hotel de la Poste is a superb, classic dish. The scallops are first cooked in white wine perfumed with juniper berries, fennel and lemon; they are then covered with an egg-and-cream sauce flavoured with mushrooms and tomato, and either served in gratin dishes or scallop shells or in a brioche (M. Arama's recipe is on page 167). Since they are rich, we suggest that you serve the scallops alone as the first course of a dinner and en brioche as a supper dish. Moules marinière (page 122) or a small helping of sole Baie des Anges (page 117) would also be appropriate first courses.

For carbonnade flamande, topside of beef is first marinated in beer with onions and herbs, then browned briefly before cooking very slowly in the marinade so that the colour and flavour become rich. Plain boiled potatoes or noodles allow you to enjoy the sauce; you might also like a simple lettuce salad for some contrasting freshness.

Oeufs à la neige superimposes 'eggs' made of poached egg white on a custard made from the yolks, and tops the lot with a nest of spun sugar – not necessarily as difficult to do as it sounds. If you find the idea daunting, Cold Love (page 100) would be easier and equally suitable.

The carbonnade and the oeufs à la neige can be prepared on the morning of the party (although the spun sugar should be put on no more than two hours before dinner so that it remains crisp). You will then have all your concentration free for the coquilles St Jacques. Although M. Arama's 13-year-old son makes this dish successfully, he presumably does not have to entertain guests at the same time. It is not unduly difficult but you will have to stay in the kitchen for 20 minutes or so just before dinner, since the sauce must be watched carefully.

Wine suggestions

FIRST COURSE

EITHER	OR
white burgundy (Pouilly-Fuissé, Montagny)	Chablis (Les Clos, Fourchaume)

Both burgundies are made from the Chardonnay grape. Pouilly-Fuissé is the better wine (when from a good source), but a young Montagny is very pleasant. If you prefer Chablis, choose a *grand cru* or *premier cru* to guarantee authenticity.

MAIN COURSE

EITHER	OR
Rhône (Châteauneuf-du-Pape, Gigondas)	Portuguese red (Dão)

The carbonnade is made with beer, but you will hardly want to serve that after scallops and white burgundy. A forthright Rhône red makes a good contrast. Châteauneuf-du-Pape is a much abused name: unless you are buying from a specialist, look for a Gigondas or something similar. Otherwise, choose a reliable Portuguese blended wine.

Timetable

THE DAY BEFORE	Carbonnade flamande – prepare beef and marinate for 24 hours.
ON THE DAY	
morning	Oeufs à la neige – prepare except for spun sugar. Chill.
2½ hours before dinner	Pre-heat oven to 300°F, mark 2. Complete preparation of carbonnade flamande and put in oven.
1½ hours before	Coat oeufs à la neige with spun sugar.
1 hour before	Prepare everything for coquilles St Jacques.
20 mins before	Cook coquilles St Jacques.
¼ hour before	Parsley potatoes – put potatoes on to cook. Chop parsley.
Between courses	Turn potatoes in parsley and butter.

Coquilles St Jacques, Hotel de la Poste

Hotel de la Poste, Swavesey
chef/proprietor: André Arama

12 scallops
1 large onion
¼ lb butter
10 juniper berries
10 fennel seeds
1 slice of lemon
salt, pepper
¼ pint white wine
4 fl oz cold water
4 sprigs parsley
½ teasp sugar
1 small onion or shallot
1 teasp chopped parsley
3 oz mushrooms
1 teasp tomato puree
¼ pint double cream
2 egg yolks
a squeeze of lemon juice
nutmeg (optional)

Wash the scallops in cold water, remove any discoloured parts and separate the coral. (If the scallops are large, they may be halved.)

Slice the large onion and sweat it in a covered pan with an ounce of butter and a pinch of salt. When it is cooked but not browned, remove the pan from the stove, and arrange the scallops and coral over the onion. Add the crushed juniper berries, fennel, lemon slice, salt, pepper, wine, cold water, an ounce of butter, the parsley sprigs and the sugar. Bring to the boil, reduce the heat and simmer very gently for 10 minutes.

In a different pan, melt an ounce of butter with the finely chopped small onion or shallot and the chopped parsley. Fry for 3 minutes. Add the sliced mushrooms and the tomato puree and cook for a further 3 minutes. Add the strained cooking liquor from the scallops, bring it to the boil and reduce to two-thirds the original quantity. Add 4 ounces of cream and boil for 3 minutes. Mix the remaining ounce of cream with the egg yolks and a tablespoonful of white wine. Add to the sauce, whisking firmly, and bring slowly back almost to the boil. Remove from the stove and add the last ounce of butter, a squeeze of lemon juice and a pinch of nutmeg.

Either arrange the scallops in a fireproof dish, and pour the sauce over them or put them in a brioche case (page 167).

EDITOR'S NOTE: M. Arama recommends glazing the finished dish quickly under a very hot grill, but there is a danger of the sauce 'scrambling' and you may prefer to decorate it with a little chopped parsley instead.

Carbonnade flamande

L'Escargot Bienvenu, London
chef: M. Liboi

1½ lb topside of beef
¾ lb onions
2 medium-sized carrots
bouquet garni (page 168)
¾–1 pint draught ale or equivalent
2–3 oz butter
2 oz flour (approx)
salt, pepper
1 dessertsp brown sugar
1 teasp French mustard

Cut up the beef into steaks about half an inch thick, 3 to 4 inches across. Put them in an earthenware, enamel or glass dish (not a metal one) with the sliced onions, sliced carrots, and a bouquet garni. Cover with the beer and leave to marinate for 24 hours.

Melt the butter in a frying-pan. Remove the meat from the marinade, dip it in seasoned flour and sauté until brown on both sides. Drain the onions and sauté them also until brown. Put the meat and onions in layers in a shallow stewpan or casserole. See that there is still about a tablespoonful of butter in the frying-pan. Stir in a dessertspoonful of flour to make a light brown roux (page 169), add the strained marinade and cook until it has thickened.

Stir in the brown sugar and mustard and pour the sauce over the meat. (The meat should be well covered with beer, and more may be necessary, depending on the shape of the casserole.) Simmer gently, covered, in a slow oven (300° F, mark 2) for 2½ to 3 hours.

Serve with parsley potatoes or noodles.

EDITOR'S NOTE: this dish heats up well. To vary the recipe, spread slices of French bread with French mustard and push them down in the sauce. They come to the surface and form a crisp topping during the reheating, which must be done, uncovered, at a higher temperature to brown the bread (400° F, mark 6).

Oeufs à la neige

The Bell Inn, Aston Clinton
chef: Jakob Dick

4 large or 5 medium-sized eggs
5 tablesp caster sugar
salt
$1\frac{1}{4}$ pints milk
5 tablesp vanilla sugar (page 169)

for the caramel
$\frac{1}{4}$ lb sugar
5 tablesp water

Separate the eggs, and discard one of the whites. Whisk the egg whites until they form soft peaks and then whisk in the other 5 tablespoonsful of sugar and whisk until stiff. Heat the milk in a shallow pan to just below boiling point. Scoop up some of the egg white mixture with a tablespoon, and with a second spoon smooth the top into an egg shape. Drop the 'eggs' into the simmering milk a few at a time and poach for 2 minutes. Turn them with two forks and let them poach until barely firm. Remove to a tea towel to drain.

Beat 5 tablespoonsful of vanilla sugar and a pinch of salt into the egg yolks. Pour the strained hot milk slowly onto the beaten egg yolks.

Continue stirring for a few moments until the custard thickens. Pour it into a shallow serving dish. When it has cooled a little, arrange the 'eggs' on top. Put to chill.

To finish the dessert, it should be coated with a fine golden net of spun sugar. Heat slowly 4 ounces of sugar in 5 tablespoonsful of water. When the sugar has dissolved, boil it to 310°F. This can be measured accurately with a jam thermometer; at this point the sugar is a strong golden colour but is not completely caramelized. Stand the pan in cold water to prevent the temperature rising any more; dip a wet fork into the caramel, lift it up and a thread of sugar will form which can then be spun over the 'eggs'. (If the caramel becomes hard, it may be reheated briefly.)

Winter menu 4

iced cucumber soup (6) *or* **celery and almond soup**

ballotine of duck (6), baked potatoes, leeks

toasted savoury cheese *or* **soft herring roes in white wine**

When you want to cook a meal for one of your favourite men – or all of them – there are many choices open: you can provide tomato soup and roast chicken, if those have been 'treats' since boyhood; you can spend the week's housekeeping on something normally outside your budget, like lobster or fillet steak; or you can create a meal that is special, like this one, because it needs a lot of loving preparation in the kitchen and yet makes no demands on the carver at the table. The ballotine of duck slices as easily as a loaf and it is flanked by good soups and savouries, popular with most men.

The iced cucumber soup is refreshing for several reasons: it is served cold – cooks often forget that in winter the soup may be icy so long as the dining-room is not; and the cucumber, yoghourt and cream are unexpectedly spiced with chopped gherkins, mint and garlic. The celery and almond soup, based on chicken stock, has ground almonds among the ingredients and toasted flaked ones on top. Guacamole (page 160) would be an interesting alternative to soup.

The ballotine of duck looks spectacular and tastes outstandingly good. The duck is first boned – an operation which sounds much more difficult than it actually is – and stuffed with a forcemeat of pork, veal, walnuts, apple and seasonings. Roasting by some magic restores its shape, and it is then served in thick slices with an apricot sauce that has been spiced with cinnamon and ginger. (Once you have mastered the technique of boning the duck you will probably want to invent new stuffings and sauces of your own, or try similar methods with a chicken or turkey for a buffet party.) Plain baked potatoes and leeks will counter the sweet richness of the duck.

Grilled tomatoes and crisped rings of Spanish onion enliven the toasted savoury cheese. For the second savoury, poached herring roes are served in a cream and wine sauce. If you prefer a sweet, orange caramel trifle (page 32) or orange and lemon charlotte (page 50) would be possible.

135

It is worth boning the duck when you have plenty of time to spare so that you do not feel rushed. (It may take you an hour the first time, but Mr Dupays suggests a target of half an hour once you are expert.) It could be both boned and stuffed on the morning of the party. The soups could also be made ahead of time, and the initial preparations for either savoury could be made before dinner, although the toasted cheese should be finished after the main course.

Wine suggestions

MAIN COURSE	EITHER	OR
	Gewürztraminer	Rioja

Since the sauce with the ballotine of duck is fairly sweet, you might find the Gewürztraminer (spicier than Traminer) appropriate. If you prefer a red wine, do not choose a great one, which would have to compete with the sauce, but something soft with an undertone of sweetness.

SAVOURY	EITHER	OR
	white port, Sercial Madeira	late-bottled port

Any of these would be perfectly suitable here. Let the tastes of the person you are cooking for decide.

Timetable

THE DAY BEFORE — Celery and almond soup – make chicken stock.
Duck – make veal stock for sauce.

ON THE DAY
morning — *either* Make iced cucumber soup, and put to chill
or Make celery soup; do not add toasted almonds.
Duck – bone and stuff.

1½ hours before dinner — Pre-heat oven to 375°F, mark 5.
1¼ hours before — Put ballotine of duck and potatoes in the oven.
Duck – make apricot sauce.

¾ hour before — Toasted savoury cheese – make sauce; prepare ingredients.

20 mins before — Cook leeks.
¼ hour before — Soft roes in wine – prepare and keep warm in a bain-marie.

10 mins before — Celery and almond soup – toast almonds.
last minute — Cucumber soup – add mint and decorate.
Celery soup – add toasted almonds.
Put apricot sauce to reheat gently.

after main course — Savoury cheese – mix ingredients and grill.

Iced cucumber soup (6)

The Empress, London
chef: Gino Scandolo

1 very large, or 2 small cucumbers
¼ pint double cream
¼ pint yoghourt
¼ pint soured cream
1 or 2 cloves garlic
3 cocktail gherkins
2 tablesp tarragon vinegar
salt, pepper
2 tablesp chopped mint
a few shrimps, prawns or pearls
    of salmon roe (optional)

Wash the cucumber and, still unpeeled, grate it fairly coarsely. Stir in the cream, yoghourt and soured cream. (The combinations or proportions of these can be varied.) Crush the garlic and chop the gherkins very finely. Mix them in, also the vinegar, salt and pepper.

Put the soup in the refrigerator until it is well chilled.

Just before serving, stir in the chopped mint. If the consistency seems too thick, add a few ice cubes or a little milk. Spoon into goblets or small bowls; as a final touch, each one can be decorated with a few shrimps, prawns or pearls of salmon roe.

Brown bread (page 166) and butter, or hot rolls go well with this soup.

Celery and almond soup

Rothay Manor, Ambleside
chef: Bronwen Nixon

1 medium-sized, or ½ a large head
    of celery
1 medium-sized carrot
1 medium-sized onion
1 medium-sized leek
1 oz butter or dripping
salt, pepper
2 pints chicken stock (page 171)
bouquet garni (page 168)
1 oz ground almonds
¼ pint milk
½ oz flaked almonds
whipped cream

Clean all the vegetables and chop them roughly. Melt the fat and soften the vegetables in it for about 10 minutes in a covered saucepan with some salt and pepper, shaking frequently.

Add the stock and a bouquet garni and simmer for an hour. Remove the herbs and put the vegetables and stock through the liquidiser. Add the ground almonds and the milk. The soup should be a good consistency at

this stage but if it is too thin, thicken it with a little cornflour mixed with cold milk. Check the seasoning.

Put the flaked almonds on a baking tray in a moderate oven (350°F, mark 4). Stir or shake them frequently so that they do not burn but turn an even golden colour.

Sprinkle some almonds on top of each helping with a blob of whipped cream.

Ballotine of duck (6)

The Priory, Bath
chef: John Dupays

1 duck, about 3 lb dressed weight

for the forcemeat
½ lb lean pork
½ lb stewing veal
2 oz fresh breadcrumbs
2 sticks celery
2 oz walnuts
1 large cooking apple, peeled and
  cored
1 medium-sized onion
2 tablesp chopped parsley
½ teasp fresh or dried sage
salt, pepper
3 fl oz sherry

for the sauce
1 tin apricots (about 15 oz)
¼ pint veal stock
3 fl oz madeira
¾ teasp ginger
½ teasp cinnamon
salt, pepper

The duck must first be boned. The aim is to detach the flesh and skin from the bones without breaking the skin except at the back where the bird has to be opened first. Be careful always to keep the cutting edge of the knife facing bone, not flesh.

Slit the duck along its back from neck to tail, exposing the backbone. With a small very sharp knife or scissors, cut the flesh away from the carcase down one side, pulling it from the bone gently. At the joints of the legs and wings, cut through the ball joint itself so that the leg and wing come away with the flesh.

Continue cutting down the carcase until the top of the breast bone is reached where the skin and flesh are very thin. Turn the bird and work down the other side in the same way as far as the ridge of the breast bone. Cut very carefully along the ridge. Chop off the wings at the first joint. Open the skin out and, working from the inside, scrape the flesh from the bones of the legs and wings so that the bones can be pulled out. The duck is now ready to stuff. If any cuts have accidentally been made in the skin, sew them up with a needle and strong thread.

For the forcemeat, mince together the pork and veal, then add the breadcrumbs, the celery, walnuts, apple, onions, parsley and sage, all roughly chopped, with the salt, pepper and sherry. Mix well together and form it into a sausage shape. Spread the duck, skin side down, and put the stuffing in the centre. Wrap the skin firmly round the forcemeat, tucking the neck and vent ends in first. Sew up the skin with fine string along the back, then press the duck into shape. Place it on a rack over a roasting tin in a moderately hot oven (375°F, mark 5), and roast it for 1½ hours, turning it over every 20 minutes.

For the sauce, sieve or liquidise the apricots, with the syrup. Stir in the remaining ingredients. Heat the sauce gently.

Place the duck on a carving dish, decorated with watercress or parsley, and carve it in thick slices, one per person. Serve the sauce separately.

EDITOR'S NOTE: some Chinese cookery books – for example, the Time-Life *Chinese Cookery* – have clear diagrams of how to bone a duck using a slightly different method.

Toasted savoury cheese

Bumbles, London
chef: David Prentice

1 oz butter
1 tablesp flour
5 tablesp milk
6 oz Cheddar cheese
salt, pepper
4 slices white bread, toasted
1 Spanish or French onion
English mustard
1 tablesp olive oil
2 tomatoes

Melt the butter and stir in the flour. Cook for a minute or two and blend in the milk. Stir well over the heat until the sauce has thickened before adding 4 ounces of the grated cheese. Season the sauce with salt and freshly ground black pepper and spread a little on each slice of toast. Grill them lightly.

Slice the raw onion thinly into rings and mix it lightly with the remaining 2 ounces of cheese, a little mustard, olive oil, seasoning and the tomatoes, skinned and chopped. Pile this on top of the cheese sauce and put under a hot grill until the top is pale brown and crisp. Serve very hot.

Soft herring roes in white wine

Lockets, London
chef: Franz Naotrsek

1 lb soft herring roes
lemon juice
2 small shallots
4 tablesp dry white wine
4 fl oz double cream
salt, pepper

Clean the roes, and put them in a pan with enough slightly salted water to cover them, and a little lemon juice. Poach them in this water for 2 minutes, then drain them.

Chop the shallots, put them in a frying-pan with the wine and boil until the wine is reduced to a table-spoonful. Stir in the cream, add the roes and simmer them gently for about 5 minutes until they are cooked and the sauce has thickened. Season with salt and freshly ground black pepper before serving.

This dish will keep hot, covered, in a bain-marie (page 168).

Winter menu 5

avocado mousse aux crevettes *or* **Snaffles mousse (6)**

venison pie, red cabbage, petits pois

angel pie (6)

This menu's main course calls for hearty appetites and the meal would be an excellent one to serve to friends after an afternoon outdoors.

The avocado mousse has a mayonnaise-based sauce coloured (and sharpened) with tomato ketchup and Tabasco and garnished with prawns. If you serve the coffee-coloured Snaffles mousse try asking your guests to identify the ingredients: tinned consommé, cream cheese, garlic and curry powder (see *Guide* reporters' descriptions on page 142). Ratatouille (page 54) would also work as a first course, if you served some other vegetable instead of red cabbage, which is too ratatouille-like in texture.

The venison pie is made rich with salt pork and flavoured with oranges, red wine and redcurrant jelly. The crust can be puff or shortcrust pastry (page 173). Red cabbage (page 49) and petits pois will provide contrast in flavour, texture and colour and there seems no need to have potatoes when there is pastry with the meat.

Angel pie is similar to Pavlova (page 66) in its meringue base, but this time the topping is lemon curd and cream. Any other light sweet would also be suitable, as long as there were neither oranges nor apples in it to repeat the flavours of the main course.

Angel pie and Snaffles mousse could both be made on the morning of the party. The venison pie could be done in two stages, with the meat being cooked and the pastry made in the morning and the pie baked in time for dinner. The avocado mousse must not be made too early, since avocados discolour easily when they are exposed to air. (Plastic wrap pressed down onto the surface of the mousse while it is chilling will help avoid this.) The red cabbage can be cooked whenever it is convenient – even the day before if you want to be sure your house is clear of its smell – as it reheats well.

Wine suggestions

	MAIN COURSE	EITHER	OR
		burgundy (Côte de Nuits: Vosne-Romanée, Nuits-St-Georges)	Barolo

The splendid venison pie deserves a wine which will match it. Either a good full burgundy or Barolo, both of some age, have the necessary weight and smoothness. Open the Barolo 2–3 hours beforehand.

Timetable

THE DAY BEFORE — Prepare and cook red cabbage.

ON THE DAY
morning — Venison pie – cook meat; make pastry and rest it in the refrigerator.
Make Snaffles mousse.
Make angel pie but do not add whipped cream.

$1\frac{1}{2}$ hours before dinner — Avocado mousse – prepare, cover and chill.

$\frac{3}{4}$ hour before — Venison pie – complete preparation.

$\frac{1}{2}$ hour before — For shortcrust pastry – pre-heat oven to 400°F, mark 6.
For puff pastry – pre-heat oven to 425°F, mark 7.
Whip cream for angel pie.

$\frac{1}{4}$ hour before — Venison pie – put in oven.
Red cabbage – put in oven in a bain-marie.

5 mins before — Put petits pois on to cook and keep them hot.
either – For Snaffles mousse – make toast
or – For avocado mousse – prepare brown bread and butter.

just before — Reduce oven heat to 375°F, mark 5.

Avocado mousse aux crevettes

Barque and Bite, London
chef: Filippo Galante

2 large or 4 small ripe avocados
1 teasp Worcestershire sauce
salt, pepper
2 fl oz double cream
4 tablesp mayonnaise (page 171)
1 tablesp tomato ketchup
1 teasp Tabasco
lettuce leaves
¼ lb peeled prawns
watercress or lemon wedges

Skin and stone the avocados and mash the flesh in a bowl until it is smooth. Add the Worcestershire sauce and salt and pepper to taste. Whip the cream until slightly stiff and blend it into the avocados. Cover and chill for about an hour.

To make the sauce, mix together the mayonnaise, tomato ketchup and Tabasco.

Just before dinner, line glasses with the lettuce or arrange it on flat plates, spoon the avocado mixture on top, cover with the prawns and pour over the sauce. Garnish with a wedge of lemon or a sprig of watercress.

Serve with brown bread (page 166) and butter.

EDITOR'S NOTE: you may not believe that the mayonnaise can 'cool' so much Tabasco to an acceptable degree, but it does.

Snaffles mousse (6)

Snaffles, Dublin
chef/proprietor: Nicholas Tinne
This has been variously described by people who did not know what it contained as a 'creamy froth of smoked fish', 'soft, cold with liver and other flavours', 'seafood, probably mainly lobster or crab, very light and airy, exquisite and unobtrusive', 'like a savoury Guinness, smooth, creamy and garlicky'.

6 oz Philadelphia cream cheese
6 oz fl oz jellied beef consommé
or 6 fl oz beef consommé and
1 tsp gelatine
1 small clove garlic
1 small pinch curry powder
parsley, lemon

If using regular consommé, mix the gelatine with a spoonful of cold water and allow it to swell before dissolving it in the heated consommé. Let the mixture cool and proceed as above.
Put all the ingredients in a liquidiser and blend until smooth. Fill individual ramekins or other small dishes and refrigerate until set. This will be less than an hour if the consommé has been previously chilled.
Garnish with chopped parsley or a lemon wedge. Serve with hot toast.

Venison pie

The Horn of Plenty, Gulworthy
chef: Sonia Stevenson

1¼ lb stewing venison
½ lb salt streaky pork
1 tablesp fat for frying
zest of 2 oranges
1 tablesp tomato puree, or
  2 skinned, pulped tomatoes
½ bottle red wine
fresh marjoram
1 teasp arrowroot
1–2 tablesp redcurrant jelly
¾ lb puff or shortcrust pastry
  (page 173)
1 egg

Trim any fat or gristle off the venison, skin the pork and cut them into inch pieces. In a large saucepan melt the fat over a high heat, and when it is hot, put in the meat. Brown it on all sides, still over a high heat. Since it will give off quite a lot of juice, take it out when it is sealed and reduce the liquor a little. Put in the zest of the two oranges (use a good potato peeler to remove it without leaving any white pith attached). Add the tomato puree and the wine, and stir until the gravy simmers. Put the meat back into the pan, cover and simmer very slowly for 1 to 1½ hours or until it is tender.

Take a medium-sized pie dish and with a slotted spoon transfer the meat from the casserole. Stir into the remaining gravy a little fresh marjoram, a teaspoonful of arrowroot blended with a little water, and the redcurrant jelly. Taste the gravy to see how much jelly is required – this will depend on the age of the venison. If the streaky pork is very salty, no more salt will be needed.

Pour the gravy over the meat in the pie dish, diluting it if necessary in order to cover the meat, and leave to cool a little.

Roll out the pastry an inch larger than the pie dish. Cut off the extra inch all round. Damp the edges of the dish, lay on the inch strip and brush with water. Put the pastry lid in position and press the edges firmly together. Trim away any surplus pastry, then flute the edges with the back of a knife or the fingers. Make a slit in the top to allow the steam to escape. Roll out any trimmings to make decorative leaves for the top; brush it all with beaten egg.

Put the pie in the middle of a fairly hot oven (400°F, mark 6 for shortcrust; 425°F, mark 7 for puff) for about 20 minutes until the pastry is set. Brush again with the egg, reduce the heat to 375°F, mark 5, and continue to cook for 5 to 10 minutes until the pastry is well browned.

Angel pie (6)

Square and Compass Inn, North Rigton
chef: Wolfgang Stichler

for the meringue
3 egg whites
good pinch cream of tartar
5 oz caster sugar

for the filling
3 egg yolks
2 oz caster sugar
juice of ½ lemon
grated rind of 1 lemon

for decoration
¼ pint double cream

Separate the eggs and whisk the whites until they are frothy. Add the cream of tartar and continue whisking until the whites are very stiff. Fold in the 5 ounces of sugar. Butter a 7-inch flan case or pie dish and pour in the mixture. Bake in the lower half of a very slow oven (250°F, mark ½) for at least an hour until the meringue is crisp and dry. Leave to cool.

Put the yolks into a double boiler and beat them over a low heat until they start to thicken. Stir in the 2 ounces of caster sugar, the lemon juice and rind and continue to cook, stirring all the time, until the mixture has thickened. (Be careful not to let it get too hot or it will curdle.)

Leave to cool slightly before pouring it over the meringue base and spreading it in a thin layer with a spatula. Allow the pie to cool.

Whip the double cream until it is fairly thick and then fork it over the top.

Winter menu 6

pickled mushrooms *or* **avocado au gratin**

filets de porc aux pruneaux, rice, winter salad

chocolate whisky gateau (6) *or* **cheese, fruit, nuts**

The adventurous among your friends should enjoy the enterprising dishes in this full-blooded menu. It is a heavier meal than anyone would consider serving in summer but the balance of flavours and textures keeps it from becoming cloying. You might consider it for a weekend lunch if you are concerned about the digestibility of pork.

The Russian pickled mushrooms will remind you of champignons à la grecque without the olive oil. If you think them too sharp to be served alone, you could make them one of several dishes of hors d'oeuvre, with good sardines, radishes, celery or fennel as other possibilities. Whatever you serve, have plenty of French bread and butter as well. If a hot first course seems a better idea, the avocado au gratin makes a change from the avocado vinaigrette so common on restaurant menus. The avocado flesh, combined with cheese sauce and prawns, is returned to the shells and grilled.

Filets de porc aux pruneaux is a clever adaptation of the regional French dish, noisettes de porc aux pruneaux. Here, pork escalopes are beaten out, fried in butter and served with the prunes and a cream sauce. Rice to absorb the sauce and a winter salad (fennel, perhaps, if it did not appear in the hors d'oeuvre) set off the creaminess of the main dish.

Chocolate whisky gateau is a chocolate mousse, flavoured with whisky and Angostura, in a sponge case. It can be cut like a cake – in tiny helpings if necessary – and served with whipped cream. Cheese, fruit and nuts would be a sensible alternative; so would fresh fruit salad.

The pickled mushrooms can be made several days ahead, if you wish, and should have at least one day for the flavours to combine. The gateau should also be made one day ahead. The avocado shells can be filled beforehand and grilled at the last minute while you are cooking the pork. This meal will take twenty minutes of concentrated effort in the kitchen immediately before dinner, but the pork can be kept hot, covered, in a low oven while you eat the first course.

Wine suggestions

MAIN COURSE

EITHER
burgundy (Volnay),
Côtes du Rhône

OR
Pouilly-Fuissé

The suggested red wines will complement rather than fight with the porc aux pruneaux.
The dry white burgundy should be drunk young before it loses its freshness.

Timetable

A FEW DAYS BEFORE   Pickled mushrooms – prepare and seal in jars.

THE DAY BEFORE   Filets de porc – soak prunes overnight.
Make chocolate whisky gateau.

ON THE DAY
$1\frac{1}{2}$ hours before dinner   Cook prunes.
Prepare winter salad.
Chop parsley.
Prepare avocado au gratin.
Whip cream for gateau.

$\frac{1}{2}$ hour before   Pre-heat oven to 300°F, mark 2.
20 mins before   Prepare filets de porc aux pruneaux and keep them hot.

$\frac{1}{4}$ hour before   Put avocados in oven to heat.
10 mins before   Start cooking rice.
last minute   Avocado au gratin – glaze under grill.
between courses   Sprinkle pork with chopped parsley.
Toss salad.

Pickled mushrooms

Carpenters Arms, Stanton Wick
chef: Lidia Allcock
This Russian delicacy is served either as an hors d'oeuvre or as a pickle with cold meat

1 lb small button mushrooms
¼ pint white vinegar
1–3 cloves
1–2 bay leaves
6 black peppercorns

Wash the mushrooms, removing the stalks if they are large. Simmer them in hot salted water for a minute or two until they are tender.

In a separate pan, simmer the vinegar and the seasoning for 5 minutes, then leave to cool for about half an hour.

Pack the mushrooms tightly into small screw-top jars – about three ½ lb-sized ones should be sufficient. Pour the vinegar mixture over to cover the mushrooms. Seal the jars. The mushrooms will keep for several days.

EDITOR'S NOTE: if you find the taste too sharp, add a little olive oil to each portion when serving.

Avocado au gratin

Frederick's, London
chef: D. Jamard

½ pint thick bechamel sauce
  (1 oz butter, 1 oz flour, ½ pint
  milk – page 174)
2 large avocados
¼ lb shelled prawns
pepper
2 oz grated Cheddar cheese (or
  half Gruyère, half Parmesan)

Make the thick béchamel sauce.

Scoop out the flesh of the avocados into a small pan and crush it with a fork. Mix in the prawns and a little freshly ground black pepper.

Stir the grated cheese into the hot béchamel sauce and add two table-spoonsful to the avocado and prawns to bind it. Heat this mixture very gently for a few minutes before filling the shells with it. Put a spoonful of the remaining sauce on top of each one and glaze them quickly under a hot grill.

EDITOR'S NOTE: if you prepare the avocados some time ahead of dinner, reheat them briefly in the oven before glazing them.

147

Filets de porc aux pruneaux

La Fringale, London
chef: Mrs I. Copus

16–20 stoned prunes
1½ lb pork fillet
3 tablesp flour
salt, pepper
2 oz butter
strip of lemon rind
¼ pint double cream
8 tablesp demi-glace (page 172)
parsley

Soak the prunes overnight.

Cook them in boiling water with a strip of lemon rind until they are soft. Drain and keep them warm.

Trim any fat off the pork fillets and slice them at an angle into 12 escalopes. Beat each one as thinly as possible – cover it with a piece of waxed paper or polythene and use a meat bat or rolling pin. Then dust the escalopes with seasoned flour. Heat the butter in a frying-pan and when it is fairly hot, fry the escalopes gently for about 5 minutes on each side.

When the escalopes are cooked, transfer them to a warm serving dish and keep them hot while making the sauce. Stir into the juices in the frying-pan the cream and the demi-glace. Add the prunes and check the seasoning. Heat together gently for a minute or two, then pour the sauce over the fillets.

Sprinkle with parsley and serve.

EDITOR'S NOTE: you may be able to find prunes which are already stoned and tenderized. Follow the cooking time given on the packet.

Chocolate whisky gateau (6)

Old Manor House, Midhurst
chef/proprietor: Robin Roake

12–16 sponge fingers or boudoir
  biscuits
¼ lb butter
¼ lb caster sugar
3 eggs
¼ lb plain cooking chocolate
2 tablesp whisky
1 or 2 drops Angostura bitters
  (optional)
whipped cream

Grease a 7-inch loose-bottomed cake tin and line it round the sides with sponge fingers – a very little soft butter smeared along their edges helps them to stick to each other and stops them falling over before the filling is put in.

Cream together the softened butter and the sugar. Separate the eggs, and whisk the yolks until they are creamy.

Beat them into the mixture. Break the chocolate into small pieces and put it, with a dessertspoonful of water, into a small saucepan (or preferably into a double boiler). When it has melted over a low heat, mix it into the butter and sugar and add one or two drops of Angostura and two tablespoonsful of whisky.

Whisk the whites of egg until they are very stiff and dry, then lightly fold them into the chocolate mixture. Pour quickly into the lined tin and chill in the refrigerator for several hours.

To serve, push the loose bottom of the cake tin up through the tin so that the dessert is still standing on its metal base. It can then be cut like a cake.

Offer whipped cream separately.

kipper pâté *or* **mackerel pâté (6)**

kidneys in Madeira, sprouts, mashed *or* **boiled potatoes**

lemon syllabub *or* **quick syllabub (8)**

With this meal you could hope equally to please foreign guests, who ought to know that we have other national dishes besides curled egg sandwiches and baked beans, and somewhat conventional British eaters who prefer to steer clear of foreign kickshaws.

Both fishy pâtés contain cream and lemon. The kipper one has whisky and Worcestershire sauce to give it bite; the mackerel pâté adds only butter, leaving the smoky flavour of the fish to dominate. Pink's fish soup (page 161) or very small stuffed aubergines (page 161) would be other good choices for the first course.

The kidney dish will almost seem like a standard mixed grill as you start to prepare it, since the kidneys are fried with bacon and mushrooms. But when the Madeira has been flamed and the cream added to the sauce, the dish suddenly leaves the breakfast table to become an elegant entrée. Plain vegetables, such as the potatoes and sprouts we suggest, are all that you need serve with this rich dish.

If you have time to make the first syllabub overleaf, you will certainly enjoy it, but the quick version is a useful last-minute alternative. Both are based on wine, cream and lemon, with brandy optional in the quick recipe and essential in the Lacy's version, since the lemon peel soaks in it overnight and releases its pungent oils. In either case, you might wish to serve shortbread biscuits, langues de chat or squares of bitter chocolate along with the syllabub.

The pâtés can be made a day ahead, the lemon syllabub could be made on either the previous day or the morning of the party. The initial preparation of the kidneys can be carried out immediately before dinner; the sauce could be completed in the kitchen or at the table if you have a chafing dish and a fireproof husband.

Wine suggestions

APERITIF AND FIRST COURSE	EITHER	OR
	white Hermitage	Gewürztraminer or Alsace Riesling

The Hermitage, at least when it is over six years old, has a strong enough character to match the smoked fish pâtés. The Riesling will be dry, full-flavoured and clean. The Gewürztraminer is less dry, but equally capable of holding its own.

MAIN COURSE	EITHER	OR
	claret (Pomerol, St Emilion)	burgundy (Morey-St-Denis)

It is difficult to find a partner for kidneys cooked with cream and Madeira. A fairly full wine is indicated. The Pomerols and St Emilions described on page 97 would not be overwhelmed by the dish, nor would the powerful Morey-St-Denis from the Côte de Nuits, which also deserves its place in this book as a favourite wine of Raymond Postgate's.

Timetable

TWO DAYS BEFORE	Lemon syllabub – steep rind in brandy.
THE DAY BEFORE	Make either fish pâté and chill overnight. Lemon syllabub – make and chill overnight.
ON THE DAY	
1 hour before dinner	Make quick syllabub and chill it.
$\frac{1}{2}$ hour before	Kidneys in Madeira – prepare ingredients and fry.
$\frac{1}{4}$ hour before	Pre-heat oven to 350°F, mark 4. Put potatoes on to cook.
5 mins before	Put sprouts on to cook.
just before	For either fish pâté – make toast. Put kidneys in the oven.
between courses	Kidneys - complete the preparation.

Kipper pâté

Bowlish House, Shepton Mallet
chefs: Miss Hall and Miss Oakes

½ lb kipper fillets, fresh or frozen
1 tablesp melted butter
juice of ½ small lemon
2 dessertsp whisky
2 tablesp double cream
Worcestershire sauce
Tabasco
pepper
clarified butter (page 168)

Cook, skin and remove the worst of the bones from the kipper fillets. Melt a tablespoonful of butter, add it to the fillets, and put them together with the lemon juice and whisky into a liquidiser. Blend to a smooth paste. Stir in the cream and season to taste.

Press into a dish or individual ramekins and pour melted, clarified butter over.

Serve with hot toast and butter.

This will keep for at least a week in the refrigerator.

Mackerel pâté (6)

The Horn of Plenty, Gulworthy
chef: Sonia Stevenson

2 smoked mackerel
½ lb butter (approx)
½ pint cream (approx)
juice of a lemon
salt, pepper

Skin and bone the mackerel and put it in the liquidiser. Heat the butter until it is quite hot and add just enough of it to enable the fish to 'turn' in the liquidiser to form a puree. When it is smooth, tip it into a bowl and mix into it the cream and lemon juice – according to taste. For a sharp-tasting pâté, increase the amount of lemon juice, and for a milder flavour use more cream. Put into a pâté dish or individual dishes and chill.

Serve in the dishes or arrange separate helpings on lettuce leaves accompanied by hot brown toast.

CHEF'S NOTE: this recipe works equally well with kippers. The given quantities make about enough for six but this will of course depend on the size of the mackerel. How much butter to add also depends on the size of the fish. The fresher and juicier the mackerel are, the better.

Kidneys in Madeira

Cleeveway Hotel, Bishop's Cleeve
chef: John Marfell

1 lb lamb's kidneys
¼ lb streaky bacon
¼ lb onion
6 oz button mushrooms
2 oz butter
salt, pepper
3 tablesp Madeira
4 tablesp double cream

Peel and trim the kidneys and slice them in half. Dice the bacon and onions and cut the mushrooms into slices.

Heat the butter in a sauté pan, and fry the chopped bacon and onion. Move it to the side of the pan and put in the pieces of kidney, cut side facing down.

Fry quickly on both sides for a few minutes, then add the mushrooms and salt and pepper. Cook gently for a few minutes, then cover the pan with buttered paper or a lid and put it in a moderate oven (350°F, mark 4) for about 12 minutes.

Return the pan to the heat on the top of the stove. Warm the Madeira in a ladle or pan, then pour it over the kidneys and set fire to it. Let it cook for a minute or two before stirring in the cream. Check the seasoning.

Lemon syllabub

Lacy's, London
chef: Bill Lacy

1 lemon
brandy
3 oz caster sugar
½ pint double cream
scant ½ pint sweet white wine
blanched strips of lemon rind

Peel the lemon thinly, using a potato peeler. Squeeze out the juice and put it in a small bowl with the rind and enough brandy to make ⅛ pint. Leave overnight. Strain and add the sugar to the liquid. Stir until it has dissolved. Whip the cream with a balloon whisk until it just holds its shape.

Gradually add the brandy and lemon juice mixture and the wine. The cream should absorb it all and still stand up in soft peaks, but it must be added only a very little at a time, with continuous beating, to be sure of success. Pile into little cups or glasses. Chill at least overnight, although the syllabub will keep in the refrigerator for several days.

Sprinkle a few blanched strips of lemon rind in a little cluster on top before serving.

Quick syllabub

Thornbury Castle, Thornbury
chef/proprietor: Kenneth Bell

½ pint double cream
2 lemons
2–4 oz caster sugar
a small glass of sherry,
   Sauternes or brandy

Beat the cream and grated rind of one lemon. As it thickens, add the juice of both lemons and the sugar. Beat until it holds its shape. Adjust the balance of lemon juice and sugar if necessary. Flavour with the wine or brandy (or wine and brandy).

Serve in small glasses or pots. Chill for about an hour before serving.

terrine de canard aux raisins de Corinthe (16)

matelote bourgeoise, watercress and fennel salad

ice-cream, butterscotch sauce (8–10), mint chocolate sauce (6)

Even Scrooge finally gave a party at Christmas time. If you wish to entertain during the last week of the year without actually giving a formal dinner, whether Christmas or otherwise, you might like the idea of inviting more friends than your table can hold, for a buffet supper which can be eaten with equal comfort sitting or standing. It would be an enjoyable party for Christmas Eve, provided you did not have to cook an enormous dinner the next day.

The duck terrine is not only appropriate to the season, but also an incentive to give a large party, since it requires a whole duck and makes enough for about 16 people. In Normandy it is sometimes served to visitors with a glass of port, and the slight sweetness which it takes from the rum and currants makes this a happy combination. It can be prepared a day ahead, or even more.

Matelote bourgeoise is another rich dish (given here, as usual, in quantities for four). It uses the traditional red wine in its rich brown sauce, along with mixed fish, vegetables, onions and mushrooms. If you follow our suggestions for the accompanying wine, you will be interested to find that this is one case where fish doesn't make red wine taste of iron filings. Although this recipe is expensive for large numbers, you could economise by changing the proportions of dearer to cheaper fish. The stew can be prepared ahead and reheated with its lid of croûtes just before it is needed. The fennel and watercress salad will provide a refreshing and interesting contrast to the rich sauce. Nuts and cheese will probably be enough for many of your guests, but for the hardy, there are two sauces for ice-cream, the butterscotch one to be served hot, the mint chocolate one either hot or cold.

The pâté should be flanked by baskets of French and one other kind of bread, which will also serve if you have cheese later. The stew will keep hot if it is in a deep pot (over a hot-plate if you have one) and is served in bowls rather than on flat plates, which are difficult to balance. Some people might dunk bread instead of spooning up the sauce, but you should have soup spoons handy in case they are needed as well as forks. People should be encouraged to help themselves to the sauces with the ice-cream, and you may decide to put out dishes of flaked toasted almonds, broken walnuts, candied fruits, or other garnishes for the ice-cream. Once again, deep dishes rather than flat ones will avoid spills.

Wine suggestions

APERITIF AND
FIRST COURSE

EITHER OR

white port   Chambéry vermouth
The sweetness in the duck pâté goes well with
chilled white port. Vermouth, and, if you can
find it, the strawberry-scented pink Chambéryzette
would also be pleasant.

MAIN COURSE

EITHER OR

Beaujolais   Rhône (red Hermitage)
A better version of the cooking wine would suit
here, with a young Beaujolais (even Beaujolais de
l'année, obtainable before Christmas) or a more
mature Rhône to match the heavy fish stew.

Timetable

THE DAY BEFORE

Make terrine de canard.

ON THE DAY
morning

Make matelote bourgeoise and refrigerate.
Make sauces for ice-cream.

1 hour before dinner

Take matelote from refrigerator.
Prepare croûtes.
Prepare watercress and fennel salad.

¾ hour before
½ hour before
just before

Pre-heat oven to 350°F, mark 4.
Put matelote to reheat with croûte topping.
Butterscotch sauce – leave to reheat gently.
Mint chocolate sauce – leave to heat in a double
boiler if desired.
Toss salad.

Terrine de canard aux raisins de Corinthe (16)

Bistro Angeline, Salem
Mrs Jacob says that this dish is commonly served at Christmas in Normandy and other parts of France where ducks are plentiful

3½-lb duck, dressed weight
1 lb belly of pork
6 oz currants
6 fl oz rum
½ lb stewing veal
liver from the duck, plus one
   more, or 1 or 2 chicken livers
2 eggs
salt, pepper
½ lb streaky, unsmoked bacon
bay leaf
thyme
4 tablesp flour

Roast the duck (page 162). Put the belly of pork in a small roasting tin or ovenproof dish and roast it at the same time but take it out after an hour. While the duck is cooking and cooling, put the currants to soak in half the rum.

When the duck has cooled, remove the breast fillets carefully with a sharp knife and put them to marinate with the rest of the rum while preparing the terrine.

Strip the remaining flesh from the duck and discard the skin. Remove any bones from the belly of pork and cut it into pieces. Mince the duck, the pork, the uncooked veal and the livers. Put them all in a good-sized mixing bowl and add the currants and their marinade, two well-beaten eggs, salt and pepper.

Mix all these together thoroughly.

Line two medium-sized terrines with pieces of bacon, then half fill each one with a quarter of the mixture. Take the breasts of duck out of their marinade and slice them horizontally in two. Place the two halves in a layer in each dish, then cover with the rest of the mixture. Pour the rum marinade over and put another piece of bacon on top with a bay leaf and a sprig of thyme. Put the lids on the terrines and seal them down with a flour and water paste.

Put the dishes into a bain - marie (page 168), in a fairly slow oven (325°F, mark 3) and cook for 2 hours.

Allow the dishes to cool before removing the seal from the lids, then chill the terrines overnight.

Matelote bourgeoise

Romans, Silchester
Louis Bielski, the chef, adapted this recipe from the one in the original edition of
Tante Marie's French Kitchen

¾ lb cheap white fish (cod, hake,
  whiting)
4–6 oz firm fish (sole, trout,
  halibut)
2–3 oz shrimps or prawns
  (or a mixture)
1 oz flour (approx)
3 tablesp butter
16 shallots or pickling onions
6 oz mushrooms
¾ bottle red wine
chopped parsley
1 medium-sized onion
1 medium-sized carrot
sprig of thyme
2 strips lemon peel
sprig of rosemary
1 large clove garlic
salt, pepper

for garnishing
fried croûtes
shrimps
parsley

Cut the fish into bite-sized pieces,
pass them through flour and fry
quickly in the butter. Remove the
fish and put the chopped shallots
in the pan, with a little additional
butter if necessary. Cover the pan
and cook slowly until the shallots are
almost soft. Add the quartered
mushrooms and cook for another
five minutes.

Meanwhile, in a large saucepan,
simmer the wine, the parsley, the
finely chopped onion, the carrot in
rounds, the herbs and the seasoning,
for 30 minutes. Add the fish to the
shallots and mushrooms, pour in the
strained wine and simmer till the

sauce is thickened. Pour into individual earthenware dishes or one larger
one and refrigerate if the dish is not
to be cooked immediately.

Cut heart-shaped or circular pieces
of white bread (using biscuit cutters
or the rim of a tumbler) and fry them
till golden in a mixture of olive oil
and butter. Arrange them on top
of the stew and heat in the oven.
Before serving, garnish with a few
fried shrimps and chopped parsley.

EDITOR'S NOTE: since the sauce is so
flavoursome, this dish could be made
for everyday meals with cheap fish
alone.

Butterscotch sauce (8-10)

Miners' Arms, Priddy
chef/proprietor: Paul Leyton

6 oz butter
3 tablesp golden syrup
1 lb demarara sugar
1 15-oz tin full-cream evaporated
  milk

Put the butter to melt in a saucepan over a low heat but do not let it burn. Add the syrup and sugar and stir until the sugar has melted and all are blended well together. Pour in the evaporated milk and beat well to combine all the ingredients.

The sauce can be made beforehand and heated when required; if it is to be used immediately, increase the flame a little and stir until the sauce is very hot.

Pour a little over individual portions of home-made ice-cream, or hand it separately.

CHEF'S NOTE: this sauce keeps well and if any is left, it can be stored in a screw-top jar and reheated. Alternatively it can be used as the filling for a flan case – with a topping of whipped cream or coconut or bread-crumbs or crushed cornflakes.

Mint chocolate sauce (6)

The French Partridge, Horton
Mr Partridge, the chef-proprietor, suggests that this sauce also goes well with profiteroles – puffs of choux pastry filled with whipped cream

6 oz plain chocolate
3 oz caster sugar
½ pint double cream
a tiny drop of oil of peppermint

Break the chocolate into small pieces and put it into a small saucepan with two dessertspoonsful of water. Heat it very gently, stirring it occasionally until the chocolate has melted into a smooth cream. Stir in the sugar, the cream, and the peppermint essence and bring the sauce to the boil.

Pour it into a dish or sauceboat and serve it, hot or cold, with home-made ice-cream.

EDITOR'S NOTE: oil of peppermint can be bought in the chemist's and is also useful for toothache if you run out of whisky.

Additional recipes

Fresh herring pâté (6)

Pink's, Fairford
chef/proprietor: Susan Kennaway

4 herrings, weighing about
  ½ lb each, unfilleted
1 teasp flour
1 large egg yolk
1 teasp anchovy essence or 2
  teasp anchovy paste
2 teasp chopped parsley
2 teasp chopped chives
½ teasp salt
freshly ground black pepper

The fish for this pâté is minced when raw; thus the flesh has first to be separated from the skin and bones. It is a lengthy process to remove as many of the tiny bones as possible, and not one for the squeamish. Slit open the herrings and with the point of the knife, ease off the centre bone and as many of the smaller bones as possible. Scrape off the flesh from the skin, and put it through the finest blade of the mincer twice. Beat in all the other ingredients until the pâté is well mixed.

Pack it into a buttered terrine or small oblong baking tin, cover it and set it in a bain-marie (page 168) to cook in a medium oven (325°F, mark 3) for 1½ hours.

Remove the lid to cool it, re-cover and chill in the refrigerator for a few hours or overnight. It will then cut into slices – like a meat terrine – and can be served with brown bread (page 166) and butter.

Highbullen's guacamole

Highbullen Country House Hotel, Chittlehamholt
chef: Mrs Neil

2 ripe avocados
1 clove garlic
juice of ½ lemon
1 tablesp grated onion
2 tomatoes
4–6 black olives
dash of Tabasco
salt, pepper
½–1 teasp chilli powder
2 tablesp (approx) mayonnaise
  (page 171)
lettuce

Peel the avocados and slice them into a mortar or a small, heavy bowl, rubbed with the garlic. Pound the flesh until it is smooth, and then add to it the lemon juice, the grated onion (with the juice drained off), the skinned, deseeded and chopped tomatoes, the chopped olives, the Tabasco, salt, pepper and chilli powder. Cover with a thin layer of mayonnaise to prevent discolouring.

Just before serving, stir in the mayonnaise, and serve in a bowl or on a lettuce leaf.

EDITOR'S NOTE: Highbullen serves potato chippings as a garnish; you could use any plain, savoury biscuit or strips of raw vegetable for dipping. (For the chippings, soak coarsely grated potato in salted water for 30 minutes. Dry and fry in deep fat until crisp and golden. Drain well.)

Pink's fish soup (4-6)

Pink's, Fairford
Susan Kennaway says one can make this soup with any white fish

1 lb white fish
2 pints chicken stock (page 171)
¼ pint olive oil
3 large onions
½ clove garlic
3 oz tomato puree
2 lb tomatoes
1 bay leaf
1 teasp sweet paprika
salt, pepper
chopped parsley

Cook the fish gently in a little of the stock. Flake it, taking care to remove all the skin and bones.

Heat the oil in a large saucepan and in it fry gently the finely chopped onions and garlic until they are transparent. Add the tomato puree, the strained stock, the peeled, de-seeded and chopped tomatoes, the bay leaf and the paprika. Simmer for 20 minutes.

Add the fish, bring the soup slowly back to just below boiling point and check the seasoning. Serve it garnished with finely chopped parsley.

CHEF'S NOTE: if the soup is not rich enough in colour, add a little more tomato puree.

Stuffed aubergines au gratin

Country Fare, Buckfastleigh
chef: John Stewart

2 large or 4 small aubergines
salt
2½ oz butter
2 oz olive oil
¼ lb chopped onion
¼ lb mushrooms
1 large clove garlic
1 bay leaf
a good pinch sweet basil
1 teasp finely chopped parsley
pepper
4 large skinned tomatoes
¼ pint béchamel sauce (page 174)
2 tablesp grated Gruyère,
   Parmesan or strong Cheddar
2 tablesp fresh breadcrumbs

Cut the aubergines in two length-ways. Without damaging the skins, make cuts across the exposed surfaces, sprinkle them with salt and leave until beads of moisture appear.

Heat 2 ounces of the butter and oil in a large shallow pan. Pat the aubergines dry, and cook them gently cut side down until the skins go brown. Remove them from the pan and add the finely chopped onion. Add, more oil if required and cook fairly quickly but without browning.

When they are partly cooked, add the chopped mushrooms and garlic, the herbs and seasoning. Continue cooking, but covered, for about 5 minutes, then add the chopped tomatoes.

Mix the vegetables, and continue cooking for another 5 minutes.

Meanwhile take the aubergines and scoop out the pulp; add it to the pan.

Mix and cook for a little longer. Remove the bay leaf, taste and adjust the seasoning. If the stuffing is too moist, a little cooked rice or fresh breadcrumbs may be added.

Fill the aubergine shells with the mixture and place them in a buttered ovenproof dish. Coat each one lightly with béchamel sauce to which 2 tablespoonsful of the cheese has been added. Fry the rest of the breadcrumbs in $\frac{1}{2}$ oz butter, mix with the grated cheese and sprinkle on top of the aubergines. Bake in a very hot oven (450°F, mark 8) for long enough to set the gratin.

Roast duck

Howard Arms, Ilmington
chef/proprietor: W. T. Last

A duckling of just over 5 lb weight when undrawn, and about $3\frac{1}{4}$ lb when dressed, will serve four people. Allow 20–25 minutes per pound (dressed weight) roasting time. There are at least two schools of thought on the way to roast a duck, though each aims to extract as much fat as possible from the skin and the subcutaneous layer beneath, and make the skin crisp and golden. This is done either by cooking rather more moderately (350/375°F, mark 4/5) than the term 'roasting' suggests, with the bird sitting on an oven rack so that the fat slowly drips away into a roasting tin below. Or the cooking is started at roasting temperature (425°F, mark 7) to brown the bird lightly for the first 15 minutes, and later reduced to a more moderate heat (350°F, mark 4).

At the Howard Arms, the cooking is done on a solid fuel stove and thus the slow method is used. The bird is cooked breast-down for the first hour; its skin is crisped in the top oven at the end. It is basted with a little cold water at this stage, and even coloured with a little honey if it has not turned quite golden enough.

Before roasting, prick the skin over the breast and legs to let out the fat as it cooks, put a peeled and quartered onion inside, and sprinkle inside and out with salt and pepper.

The juices will run a clear yellow when the duck is cooked. It will not do it any harm if you allow it to 'rest' for 15 minutes after it is cooked, in the oven with the door ajar.

Chicken chanfaina

4–6 chicken joints
3 oz butter
2 tablesp cooking oil
2 medium-sized onions
2 cloves garlic
¼ lb mushrooms
1 medium-sized aubergine
½ lb tomatoes, fresh or tinned
2 green peppers
2 courgettes
salt, pepper
½ pint red wine

Panos, London   chef: P. Kyziacou

Sauté the chicken in the heated butter and oil in a flameproof casserole or medium-sized sauté pan until it is brown all over.

Add the chopped vegetables and sauté them briefly before seasoning them and adding the red wine. Bring gently to the boil, cover and simmer for between 25 and 35 minutes until the chicken is tender.

Transfer to a heated serving dish and serve with new potatoes or potatoes *à la parisienne*. (These are potato balls scooped out with a vegetable scoop, cooked gently in butter until they are golden brown, then rolled either in meat jelly or chopped parsley.)

Moussaka

3 medium-sized aubergines
¾ lb onions
½ pint olive oil (approx)
1–1¼ lb finely minced raw
   beef or lamb
pinch of cinnamon
3 tablesp chopped parsley
½ teasp sugar
1 crushed clove of garlic
salt, pepper
7 fl oz stock (page 170)
1 dessertsp tomato paste
½ pint béchamel (page 174)
4 tablesp grated cheese
   (preferably Parmesan)

White Tower, London   chef: Luigi Contini

Cut the aubergines into slices (about ¼-inch thick). Salt and put aside for about an hour. Wash and dry them. Fry them gently in olive oil until they are soft. Remove them and add the finely chopped onions with more oil if necessary. When they begin to colour, add the meat, cinnamon, parsley, sugar and garlic and cook until the meat has browned.

Cover the bottom of an ovenproof dish with a layer of aubergines followed by a layer of meat. Continue to build in alternate layers, adding plenty of salt and pepper as you go. Finish with a layer of aubergines. (Three layers of aubergines and two layers of meat is about right.) Warm the stock and add the tomato puree to it. Pour this into the casserole and put it in a slow oven (300°F, mark 2) for about an hour, to absorb and reduce the gravy; be careful not to let it go dry.

Make the béchamel and add 3 table-spoonsful of the cheese to it. Cover the dish with the sauce, and sprinkle the rest of the cheese over it. Brown in a moderate oven (350°F, mark 4) for about 20 minutes.

EDITOR'S NOTE: before serving, drain off the excess oil from a corner of the dish with a baster or spoon.

Crêpes gruyère

Cumbrian Steak House, Keswick
chef: Michael Clark

for the pancakes
¼ lb flour
1 egg
½ pint milk
1 dessertsp butter or cooking oil
2 tablesp chopped parsley
2 tablesp chopped chives
  or 1 tablesp dried mixed herbs

for the filling
1½ oz butter
1½ oz flour
½ pint milk
1 tablesp kirsch
6 oz Gruyère

for final cooking
seasoned flour
1 egg
1 teasp oil
2 oz dried breadcrumbs
oil for deep frying

Make a pancake batter (page 172); add the herbs and allow to stand for 1–2 hours. Cook the pancakes. This mixture makes about 8 medium-sized ones – for a starter allow one each, for a supper dish, two.

Make a thick béchamel sauce (page 174) with the butter, flour and milk. As soon as the sauce is cooked, remove it from the heat and add the kirsch and the finely diced cheese. Leave to cool and get firm.

When it is cold put 2 dessertspoonsful of the mixture on the edge of each pancake. Roll it up into a smooth tube and leave to become firm – with the seam underneath. They can be cooked at once if care is taken when frying, but it is better to make them 3 or 4 hours in advance. (They will also keep in the refrigerator for up to a week.)

When it is time to cook the crêpes, heat some oil in a deep-fat pan to 375°F. While it is heating, dip each pancake roll first into seasoned flour, then into an egg which has been beaten with a little oil, and finally into breadcrumbs. The pancakes should have a complete covering of each but any excess must be shaken off.

When the oil is hot, put in the pancakes and let them fry until they are crisp and golden – 2 minutes is enough. Drain them on absorbent paper before serving.

Accompany them with a green salad, possibly containing green peppers which complement the flavour well.

Hot garlic bread

The Chanterelle, London
chef: Russell Mack

½ lb salted butter
4 medium-sized cloves garlic
1 Vienna loaf

Cream the softened butter with a wooden spoon. Using a garlic press, squeeze the garlic into the butter and mix thoroughly.

Cut the bread into 8 slices, without cutting through the base. Fan out the slices and spread both sides of each slice with the butter. Press the loaf together again and smear the top generously with more butter.

Put the loaf on a baking tray and and bake it in a moderate oven (350°F, mark 4) for half an hour. Serve very hot.

EDITOR'S NOTE: alternatively, the loaf can be wrapped in silver foil and heated in a fairly hot oven (400°F, mark 6) for 15 minutes or so. Unwrap the top for 5 minutes to allow it to become crisp. French bread can also be treated in this way. For herb bread, add a few spoonsful of finely chopped herbs – parsley, basil, chives – to the creamed butter.

Sticky toffee pudding (6)

Old Rectory, Claughton
chef: Mrs Martin

2 oz softened butter
6 oz granulated sugar
½ lb flour
1 teasp baking powder
1 egg
6 oz stoned dates
½ pint boiling water
1 teasp bicarbonate of soda
1 teasp vanilla essence
2½ oz brown sugar
1½ oz butter
2 tablesp double cream

Cream the butter and sugar together. Sift the flour and baking powder. Beat the whisked egg into the creamed mixture with a little of the flour. Continue beating for a minute or so, before mixing in the rest of the flour.

Flour the dates lightly and chop them finely. Pour the boiling water over them. Mix in the bicarbonate of soda and vanilla. Add this mixture to the batter and blend well. Turn it into a buttered cake tin (11 × 7 inches). Bake for about 40 minutes in a moderate oven (350°F, mark 4).

For the toffee coating, heat the brown sugar, butter and cream and simmer for 3 minutes. Pour over the hot pudding and place under a hot grill until it bubbles. (The coating burns easily).

Gosebery tarte

The Valley, Narberth
Miss Ruby Berry, the chef/proprietor, adapted this from a 1575 recipe in A Proper
Newe Cokerye, which suggested serving the gooseberries in a pastry 'coffin'

1 lb gooseberries
3 fl oz sweet cider or sweet
   white wine
2 thick slices white bread
2 egg yolks
2 oz butter
3 tablesp sugar
a few drops orange bitters
   (optional)
whipped cream

Top and tail the gooseberries and wash them. Put them in a pan with the cider or wine and simmer until they are half cooked. Cut the crusts off the bread and crumble it roughly. Stir the crumbs into the gooseberries and continue to stew a few minutes. Off the heat add the beaten egg yolks, butter and sugar. Add more sugar if the taste is too sharp, and a few drops of orange bitters to colour it pink. The texture should be slightly stiff: if it seems too liquid, another crumbled slice of bread can be added.

Serve it hot or cold with whipped cream piped on top.

Wholemeal bread

Ballymaloe House, Shanagarry
chef: Mrs M. Allen

1 lb wholemeal flour
¼ oz salt
1 dessertsp black treacle
1 oz fresh baker's yeast
⅛ plus ½ pint water

In a warm bowl, mix the flour and salt and warm it. Mix the treacle with ⅛ pint warm water in a small bowl, and crumble in the yeast. Put the bowl in a warm place for 7–10 minutes, until it is frothy.

Grease a bread tin and put it to warm with a tea towel.

Add the yeast mixture to the flour with the remaining ½ pint of water, also warm. Mix well. The dough will be quite wet. Put the mixture into the prepared tin, cover with the tea towel and put in a warm place to rise by about one-third or one-half its original size. (This should take about 30 minutes.)

Bake in a fairly hot oven (400°F, mark 6) for 30–40 minutes. The loaf should be nicely browned and should sound hollow when tapped on the bottom. Turn out onto a rack and cool away from draughts.

EDITOR'S NOTE: 'warm' when applied to yeast means rather less than blood heat. This bread keeps well and slices thinly.

Brioche

Hotel de la Poste, Swavesey
chef/proprietor: André Arama

½ lb flour
1 oz baker's yeast
2 tablesp water
1 teasp sugar
5 oz butter
3 standard eggs plus egg yolk
½ teasp salt

Sift 2 ounces of flour into a warm bowl, make a well in the centre and in it put the yeast and warm water. Knead into a dough, adding a little more water if necessary, sprinkle with the sugar, cover with a cloth and leave in a warm place until it has doubled in size.

In another basin or electric mixer, cream the butter. Add one egg, 5 ounces of flour, sifted, alternating with the remaining two eggs, and the salt. Mix well for 10 minutes (20 if using the mixer).

When the yeast mixture has risen (20–30 minutes), add it to the other mixture and beat vigorously for 2–3 minutes. Add the remaining ounce of flour, cover, and leave in a warm place till doubled in bulk. Tap it down to the original size, cover it and prove again in a cold place or the refrigerator.

Knead the dough with floured hands till smooth, and half-fill a buttered brioche mould. Put it in a warm place until doubled in size. Brush with egg yolk mixed with a little water. Bake at 400°F, mark 6, for about 15 minutes.

When cooked, scoop out the inside of the brioche, butter the case and put it in the oven for 5 minutes to toast.

EDITOR'S NOTE: individual brioches may be made in brioche moulds, ramekins or custard cups.

Bain-marie

A shallow pan or dish half-filled with water near simmering point, in which are placed smaller dishes or pans containing pâté, for example, or eggs, or a sauce. The bain-marie can be used on top of the stove or in the oven to keep the contents hot or cook them by indirect heat without danger of curdling or burning. An adaptation of the bain-marie is the double boiler where the inner container is suspended over the simmering water.

Bouquet garni

A bundle of aromatic herbs used to add flavour – to stocks, sauces or stews. It is composed of one or two parsley stalks, a bay leaf and a sprig of thyme. When other herbs or vegetables, such as celery leaves, are required, these are usually specified.

Tie the herbs together with a long piece of cotton or string so that they can easily be removed at the end of the cooking. If dried herbs are being used, put them in a square of muslin and tie the ends together.

Clarified butter

Butter which has been heated to separate from it the buttermilk, salt, water and any sediment it contains. These cause butter to burn when it is heated to a high temperature, as in frying. Clarified butter also keeps better and can be used for sealing the tops of pâtés.

Heat the butter gently in a heavy saucepan. When it starts to foam, skim off the top. Spoon or pour the clear butter carefully into a container, leaving the milky sediment in the bottom of the pan.

Duxelles

A preparation of minced mushroom and shallot or onion, cooked until it is dry, used for flavouring stuffings.

Chop $\frac{1}{4}$ lb mushrooms very finely and wring them out in a cloth to dry them as much as possible. Fry them in a very little butter with 2 chopped shallots or half an onion until all the liquid has evaporated and the mixture is cooked. Season. The duxelles can be made in bulk, packed into a sealed container and kept in the refrigerator.

Vanilla sugar

Sugar which has absorbed the flavour of a vanilla pod, used in the making of sweet pastry, custard, and fruit dishes.

Put one or two pieces of vanilla pod into a tightly-stoppered jar of caster sugar. After a few days the sugar will have become flavoured. The pieces of vanilla can be left in the jar and the jar topped up with fresh sugar as required; the flavour will continue to be imparted for years.

Thickening agents and methods

Roux

A blend of roughly equal weights of butter and flour, first cooked together, before the liquid is incorporated for a sauce. A roux can be described as white (for a béchamel), light brown or brown (for a demi-glace).

Melt the butter gently in a saucepan, blend in the flour and stir over heat for a minute or two to cook the flour. If a light brown roux is required cook until it starts to turn a golden colour. For a brown roux, continue until it is nut-brown. (This can be done very easily by putting the pan in a hot oven for about ten minutes.)

Beurre manié

This is also a mixture of butter and flour which is added to the liquid at the end of the cooking.

Mix to a paste equal quantities of softened butter and flour, then add it to the liquid in pieces the size of a sugar lump. Stir in each one off the heat until it has dissolved, and return the pan to the stove to allow the liquid to thicken.

Cornflour and arrowroot

Thickening agents which can be used when you do not want more fat in a sauce (or for a last minute thickening of a well-flavoured stock).

1 tablespoonful of cornflour thickens half a pint of liquid. Mix it with 2 or 3 tablespoonsful of cold water before stirring it into the hot liquid. Bring it to the boil and simmer until the sauce thickens. Continue to simmer for a few minutes to cook the cornflour. (Potato flour and rice flour are the French equivalents.) 2 teaspoonsful of arrowroot thickens half a pint of liquid. Mix as above but do not simmer once it has thickened, or the sauce will go thin again. Arrowroot gives a very clear, shiny sauce.

Egg yolk and cream

This mixture ('liaison') is used for both thickening and enriching sauces and soups at the end of the cooking.

Beat the egg yolk and cream together and blend into them a little of the hot liquid. Pour this mixture slowly back into the rest of the liquid and reheat gently. Do not allow the sauce or soup to boil or it will curdle. If the sauce must be kept hot, use a bain-marie (page 168).

Reduction

A sauce, stock or soup, can be thickened by boiling it steadily until the quantity of liquid is reduced through evaporation.

Chilling

Any sauce or soup which is chilled will become thicker than when hot, if it already has a thickening agent in it.

Stock

Brown beef stock
2 lb beef or veal bones
  or part meat and bones
1 large carrot
1 onion
1 bouquet garni (page 168) with
  celery leaves
6 peppercorns

First brown the pieces of meat, bones and sliced vegetables for 30 minutes in a roasting tin in a hot oven (425°F, mark 7). Put them with the herbs into a large saucepan with enough cold water to cover them by at least an inch (3–4 pints). Bring slowly to the boil, skim, and simmer very gently with the lid partly off for 4–5 hours. During this time skim off any scum as it rises.

Strain the stock and leave it to stand to allow the fat to rise to the surface. Remove this with a spoon or some absorbent paper, or leave the stock to get cold when the congealed fat can be removed easily.

If strongly flavoured stock is required, reduce it by boiling, before adding the seasoning.

Stock can be deep-frozen and kept for several weeks (most conveniently in pint or half pint containers), otherwise it must be re-boiled every day, or every few days if it is to be kept in the refrigerator.

Chicken stock
1 boiling fowl with giblets
(or portion, or carcase
with trimmings plus
1 lb giblets)
a piece of chopped veal bone
(optional)
vegetables and herbs as above

Prepare as for beef stock but without the preliminary browning. Simmer for only 2–3 hours. If a whole fowl is being used, remove it from the stock after the first hour, carve off the breasts and use these for any dish calling for cooked chicken (e.g. American chicken salad, page 84). Stock made from the cooked meat only, such as the remains of a roast chicken, does not taste at all the same and might impart its distinctive – and less pleasant – flavour to a delicate dish.

Mayonnaise
2 egg yolks
½ teasp salt
pepper
½ pint olive oil
lemon juice or wine vinegar

The eggs and the oil should be at room temperature. Beat the yolks with an electric beater or wooden spoon until they are thick before adding the salt and a little pepper.

Start dripping in the oil, a little at a time, beating continuously. When the mayonnaise has thickened a little, the oil can be added rather more quickly, but it is essential to start drop by drop. When half the oil has been beaten in and the mayonnaise has become very thick, whisk in some lemon juice or vinegar to thin it a little. Continue beating in the rest of the oil. Taste and add more lemon juice or seasoning if required.

If the oil is added too quickly at the beginning, or if the eggs or oil are too cold, the mayonnaise may curdle during the operation. To rescue it, start in another bowl with another egg yolk and add to it the curdled mayonnaise, teaspoonful by teaspoonful, beating continuously as before.

If the mayonnaise is to be kept for some time, or if you need to thin it for coating, whisk in 2 tablespoonsful of boiling water at the end.

Sauce tartare
2 hard-boiled egg yolks
salt, pepper
1 teasp made mustard
½ pint oil
wine vinegar or lemon juice
chopped chives or
spring onion
tarragon, parsley,
capers, gherkin

Mash the yolks in a basin and mix into them the mustard and a little salt and pepper. Start adding the oil, drop by drop, and beating it in as for making mayonnaise (above). At the end, stir in the chopped herbs. The classic French recipe for this sauce specifies chopped chives only, but other chopped herbs and pickles are frequently added.

The same herbs and pickles can be used with mayonnaise, but this gives a rather solid sauce tartare, whereas the rémoulade (with the hardboiled egg yolks) is lighter and creamier.

Demi-glace sauce
1 oz butter
1 oz flour
1 pint beef stock
1 slice unsmoked bacon
1 medium-sized onion
1 carrot
1 stick celery
1 or 2 mushrooms
2 or 3 tomatoes or puree
a few peppercorns
a bouquet garni (page 168)
2 tablesp meat jelly or
$\frac{1}{4}$ pint brown stock (page 170)
salt, pepper

A brown sauce, or sauce espagnole, enriched with strong brown stock or meat jelly, and sometimes also with Madeira. The text-book version takes 2 days to make – below is a simplified version.

Make a brown roux (page 169) and blend into it $\frac{3}{4}$ pint of the stock. Bring to the boil, stirring continuously and put to simmer gently.

Chop up the bacon and vegetables and fry them until they are brown. Add them, with the chopped tomatoes, peppercorns and the bouquet garni to the sauce and continue to simmer it, partially covered, for at least 2 hours so that it reduces. From time to time, skim off the fat which rises by adding a little of the remaining $\frac{1}{4}$ pint of cold stock, bringing the sauce back to the boil and then skimming off the top. When the sauce is reduced by at least a half, rub it through a sieve into a clean pan. Add the meat jelly. (If this is not available, reduce $\frac{1}{4}$ pint of beef stock to 2 tablespoonsful by rapid boiling.) The sauce is seasoned at the end, and a little Madeira can be added if wished.

**Vinaigrette or
French dressing**

This is an oil and vinegar dressing, seasoned with salt and pepper, in the proportions of one part of vinegar (or lemon juice) to every three of oil. You may safely increase the proportion of oil, but not that of vinegar. If a good olive oil and a good wine vinegar are used, it is unnecessary to add further flavourings but this is largely a matter of individual taste. Many people like a pinch of sugar, especially with a tomato salad.

If you wish to add other seasoning such as dry mustard, garlic, or any fresh herb (chopped parsley, chervil, tarragon or basil), mix them first with the vinegar. Those who find the flavour of olive oil too strong, may prefer to use half quantity, diluted with vegetable oil.

Batter for pancakes (crêpes)
($\frac{1}{2}$ pint)
$\frac{1}{4}$ lb flour
$\frac{1}{2}$ teasp salt
1 egg
$\frac{1}{4}$ pint milk, mixed
with $\frac{1}{4}$ pint water
$\frac{1}{2}$ oz melted butter

Sift the flour and salt into a basin. Put the egg in a well in the centre and start mixing in the milk and water a little at a time, until half has been added. Beat the batter very well at this stage until it is smooth. Add the melted butter and whisk in the rest of the liquid.

Leave the batter to stand for up to 2 hours to allow the flour to absorb the liquid – this ensures a lighter pancake.

Shortcrust pastry (6 oz)
$\frac{1}{4}$ lb flour
$\frac{1}{2}$ teasp salt
2 oz butter
2 tablesp cold
   water (approx)

Sift the flour and salt into a bowl. Cut up the butter and crumble it into the flour with the fingertips or a wire pastry mixer. Mix in enough cold water with a knife to make a firm dough, and roll it into a ball. On a floured board, stretch out the pastry bit by bit with the heel of the palm then gather it up again into a ball. Repeat this process, dust the pastry with a little flour and wrap it in buttered paper or foil. Put it in the refrigerator for up to 2 hours to firm and lose its elasticity, which would cause it to shrink during cooking.

Roll out the pastry on a floured board to the thickness of $\frac{1}{4}$–$\frac{1}{8}$ inch and about 2 inches bigger than the flan case. Grease the case and lay the pastry gently in it, pressing it down to fit the bottom and sides. Ease a little extra down the sides before cutting off the excess. Prick the bottom lightly.

If the pastry case is to be cooked empty or 'blind', line it with a piece of foil or greaseproof paper weighted with dry beans and bake it, on a baking sheet, for 10 minutes at 400°F, mark 6. Remove the paper and put the case back in the oven for another 7–10 minutes until it is lightly browned. Remove the pastry shell from its tin and cool it on a rack.

Rich shortcrust pastry
  ($\frac{1}{2}$ lb approx)
$\frac{1}{4}$ lb flour
$\frac{1}{2}$ teasp salt
$2\frac{1}{2}$ oz butter
1 small egg, or 1 yolk
$1\frac{1}{2}$–2 tablesp
  cold water

Make the pastry as described above but add the beaten egg to the flour before the water and use just enough water to bind the pastry together.

Sweet shortcrust
  pastry ($\frac{1}{2}$ lb)
$\frac{1}{4}$ lb flour
$\frac{1}{2}$ teasp salt
2 oz sugar
2 oz softened butter
1 egg yolk

Sift the flour and salt into a bowl, make a well in the centre and put the other ingredients into it. Mix them together with the fingertips and gradually draw the flour into

them until it is all incorporated. Knead the pastry lightly until it is smooth, flour and wrap it and put it in the refrigerator to chill for up to 2 hours.

Pilaff

2 oz butter
1 small onion
½ lb Patna rice
1 pint veal or chicken stock
  (page 171)
2 small tomatoes
2 tablesp cooked peas

Melt an ounce of the butter in a large saucepan and lightly colour the finely chopped onion in it. Put in the the rice, unwashed, and turn it in the butter until it is well covered. Pour the stock over the rice and cook it gently, covered, for 15–18 minutes without stirring. Check that the rice is cooked. Peel and cut up the tomatoes and stir them into the rice with the peas. Transfer to an oval serving dish and dot with the other ounce of butter.

EDITOR'S NOTE: pilaff can, of course, be made without tomatoes and peas and with all manner of additions, for example, saffron, chicken livers, mushrooms, shellfish. It can also be cooked in the oven in a casserole.

Béchamel sauce (½ pint)
  (quantities for ¾ pint given in brackets)
½ pint milk (¾ pint)
1 small onion
4 peppercorns
salt, nutmeg
¾ oz butter (1 oz)
¾ oz flour (1 oz)

(Although this white sauce can be made without flavouring the milk first, this does improve the taste.)

Bring the milk, onion and seasoning to simmering point and leave it, off the heat, for 5–10 minutes, so that the flavours can be absorbed.

Make a white roux (page 169) and blend in the milk through a strainer, a little at a time. Reheat the sauce, stirring continuously while it thickens and comes to the boil. Leave to simmer for 5–10 minutes to ensure that the flour is properly cooked. Check the seasoning.

If the sauce is to stand and be reheated later, spread a piece of buttered greaseproof paper with a hole in the middle over the surface. When you lift off the paper, the skin will come with it.

Allow ⅛–¼ pint of sauce per person.

Béarnaise sauce

5 tablesp white wine
5 tablesp tarragon vinegar
1 tablesp chopped shallot
3 egg yolks
4–5 oz butter
salt, pepper
2 tablesp chopped tarragon

Boil the white wine and the vinegar with the chopped shallots and herbs until they are reduced to 2 tablespoonsful. Allow to cool.

Beat the yolks and put them with the reduction into a double boiler (page 168) over a low heat, with the water in the bottom pan barely simmering. Add the butter a little at a time whisking in each piece lightly until it dissolves and the sauce thickens. Strain it and stir in the salt, pepper and tarragon.

The sauce must not get too hot or it will curdle. If it does, it can be rescued by whisking a few drops of cold water into it.

Equivalent temperatures and measures

Gas	Fahrenheit	Centigrade	
$\frac{1}{2}$	250°	121°	very slow
1	275°	135°	very slow
2	300°	149°	slow
3	325°	163°	warm
4	350°	177°	moderate
5	375°	190°	moderately hot
6	400°	205°	moderately hot
7	425°	218°	hot
8	450°	232°	very hot
9	475°	246°	very hot

Measures

Solids
1 kilogramme (1000 grammes) = 2 lb 3 oz (approx)
100 grammes = $3\frac{1}{2}$ oz (approx)
1 lb = 450 grammes (approx)
1 oz = 28 grammes (approx)

Liquids
1 pint = 20 fl oz = $\frac{4}{7}$ litre (approx)
1 cup (BSM) = 10 fl. oz = $\frac{1}{2}$ pint
1 gill = 5 fl oz = $\frac{1}{4}$ pint
1 litre = 35 fl oz (approx) = $1\frac{3}{4}$ pints (approx)

Handy measures
1 tablesp = $\frac{1}{2}$ fl oz (approx)
1 standard bottle of wine = 26 fl oz (approx) = 6 glasses
1 liqueur glass = 1 tablesp

Index by restaurant

England and Wales

Andalucia Restaurant, Rugby, Warwickshire
naranjas al kirsch 124
tortilla mimosa 74

Bay Horse Inn, Winton, Westmorland
cabbage with onion 36
raspberry Pavlova 66

Bay Tree Hotel, Burford, Oxfordshire
marinated kipper fillets 88

Bell Inn, Aston Clinton, Buckinghamshire
Bell Inn smokies 88
oeufs à la neige 134

Bell Inn, Ramsbury, Wiltshire
coddled pockets 128

Bistro Angeline, Salem, Carmarthenshire
terrine de campagne 45
terrine de canard 157

Bosphorus Restaurant, Penarth, Glamorgan
fasulya 75

Bowlish House, Shepton Mallet, Somerset
kipper pâté 152

Box Tree Restaurant, Ilkley, Yorkshire
cherry and almond tart 105
smoked haddock croquettes 64

Brooklands Restaurant, Dodworth, Yorkshire
casseroled pheasant 123

Carpenter's Arms, Eastling, Kent
orange curd cream 84

Carpenters Arms, Stanton Wick, Somerset
kishmish 27
pickled mushrooms 147

Central Hotel, Dover, Kent
cheesecake (American) 81
Jaegermeister pâté with Waldorf salad 108

Charlton House Hotel, Shepton Mallet, Somerset
pickled pineapple 104

Christophers, Brighton, Sussex
blackcurrant ice-cream 71

Cleeveway Hotel, Bishop's Cleeve, Gloucestershire
kidneys in Madeira 153

Country Fare, Buckfastleigh, Devon
apricot torte with almonds 61
stuffed aubergines au gratin 161

Cumbrian Steak House,
Keswick, Cumberland
   crêpes gruyère   164

Duke of York, Iddesleigh,
Devon
   Cold Love   100

Dulcinea, Weybridge, Surrey
   gazpacho   64

Elms Hotel, Abberley,
Worcestershire
   orange and lemon
   charlotte   50

Emlyn Arms Hotel,
Newcastle Emlyn,
Carmarthenshire
   pilaff   174
   turbot kebabs with
   shrimp sauce   31

Fantails, Wetheral,
Cumberland
   lemon soup   79

French Partridge,
Horton, Northamptonshire
   marrow with curry sauce 90
   mint chocolate sauce   159

Gerrans Bay Hotel,
Gerrans, Cornwall
   gooseberry meringue tart 66

Golden Cross, Wootton
Wawen, Warwickshire
   crab mousse   69

Restaurant du Gourmet,
Bristol
   scampi façon Gourmet   108

Grange Hotel, Grange-in-
Borrowdale, Cumberland
   apricot streusel   118

Gravetye Manor, East
Grinstead, Sussex
   red cabbage   49

Halland Motel & Old Forge
Restaurant, Halland, Sussex
   peach Melba   114

Hat & Feather,
Knutsford, Cheshire
   cold curried apple soup 79
   gateau Fontes   42

Highbullen Country House
Hotel, Chittlehamholt, Devon
   chocolate cream with
   maraschino   109
   Highbullen's guacamole 160

Horn of Plenty,
Gulworthy, Devon
   mackerel pâté   152
   venison pie   143

Hotel de la Poste,
Swavesey, Cambridgeshire
   brioche   167
   coquilles St Jacques,
   Hotel de la Poste   132

Howard Arms, Ilmington,
Warwickshire
   port and orange sauce   104
   prawn cocktail   69
   prune and Beaujolais
   sauce   105
   roast duck   162

Inwoods Restaurant, Five
Ashes, Sussex
   Inwoods savoury
   pancakes   98

Kildwick Hall, Kildwick,
Yorkshire
   omelette Arnold Bennett 74

Lowbyer Manor Hotel,
Alston, Cumberland
   pignatelle   35

Manor House, Gaunts
Earthcott, Gloucestershire
   pork Basil Brush   113

Marquess of Exeter,
Lyddington, Rutland
   tomato soup   93

Miners' Arms, Priddy,
Somerset
   butterscotch sauce   159

Mill House Restaurant,
Milford-on-Sea, Hampshire
   braised beef in red wine 36

Nare Hotel, Veryan,
Cornwall
   fraises Charles Stuart   56

Oak House Restaurant,
Axbridge, Somerset
   Oak House pâté   83

Old Manor House
Knaresborough,
Yorkshire
   rösti   113

Old Manor House, Midhurst,
Sussex
   chocolate whisky gateau 149

Old Priory Restaurant,
Chichester, Sussex
   stuffed tomatoes   98

Old Rectory, Claughton,
Lancashire
   sticky toffee pudding   165

Peacocks, Marlow,
Buckinghamshire
   poulet au gratin à la
   crème landaise   94

Peacock Vane, Bonchurch,
Isle of Wight
   asparagus flan   25

Pengethley Hotel, Ross-on-
Wye, Herefordshire
   Sailors' Lament   22
   spiced pears   47

Pinks, Fairford,
Gloucestershire
   fresh herring pâté   160
   Pinks fish soup   161

Poacher's Inn,
Piddletrenthide, Dorset
   leeks in cream   99
   onion cream tart   25
   orange and celery salad 127

Pool Court Restaurant,
Pool-in-Wharfedale,
Yorkshire
   involtini alla casareccia 55

Priory, Bath, Somerset
   avocado mousse   40
   ballotine of duck   138
   oranges in chocolate   124

Rising Sun, St Mawes,
Cornwall
   American chicken salad 84

Romans, Silchester,
Hampshire
   matelote bourgeoise   158
   orange caramel trifle   32
   salade niçoise   59

Rothay Manor, Ambleside,
Westmorland
celery and almond soup 137

Sharrow Bay Hotel,
Ullswater, Cumberland
chilled cream of
mushroom soup 103
strawberry pots de crème 56

Square & Compass Inn,
North Rigton, Yorkshire
angel pie 144

Swan House Hotel,
Wilmcote, Warwickshire
apple and Stilton
savoury 90

Thornbury Castle,
Thornbury, Gloucestershire
mushrooms in garlic
butter 127
quick syllabub 154

Trewince, Port Navas,
Cornwall
sole Baie des Anges 117

Valley, Narberth,
Pembrokeshire
gosebery tarte 166

White Dog, Ewhurst,
Sussex
cheesecake (Italian) 81

Wife of Bath, Wye, Kent
brown bread ice cream 37

Yew Tree Inn, Odstock,
Wiltshire
parfait au marron 129

Scotland

Clifton Hotel, Nairn,
Nairnshire
oeufs Belle Anna 45

Crusoe Hotel, Lower Largo,
Fife
salmon pâté 83

L'Etoile, Edinburgh
ratatouille 54

Houstoun House, Uphall,
West Lothian
chachouka 54

Lands of Loyal Hotel,
Alyth, Perthshire
cream of cauliflower
soup 112

Old Howgate Inn, Wester
Howgate, Midlothian
spinach soup 93

Open Arms Hotel, Dirleton,
East Lothian
chicken de Vaux 21
flummery Drambuie 129

Royal Hotel, Comrie,
Perthshire
darne de saumon de
Médicis 80

Ireland

Ardnagashel House,
Bantry, Co. Cork
ambroisie de pêches 71
caneton aux olives 65
fresh grapefruit and crab
salad 59

Ballymaloe House,
Shanagarry, Co. Cork
caramel ice cream 37
wholemeal bread 166

Snaffles, Dublin
Snaffles mousse 142

London

Barque & Bite
avocado mousse aux
crevettes 142

Au Bon Accueil
moules marinière 122

Brompton Grill
mousse au chocolat 27

Bumbles
spare ribs in honey 30
toasted savoury cheese 139

Le Carrosse
almond and watercress
soup 20
tournedos Médicis 60

Chanterelle
hot garlic bread 165

Crispins
chocolate brandy cake 22

Empress
iced cucumber soup 137

L'Escargot Bienvenu
carbonnade flamande 133

L'Etoile
ris de veau au beurre
noisette 99

Au Fin Bec
paysanne 26
steak à la moutarde 60

Le Français
coeur de filet de porc aux
herbes 70

Frederick's
avocado au gratin 147
tarte aux pommes
Joséphine 95

La Fringale
filets de porc aux
pruneaux 148

Garden
mussels in cream and
curry sauce 122
tuna and corn bisque 20

Jasper's
crème velour 109

Lacy's
lemon syllabub 154
liver with Dubonnet and
orange 41
scallop and artichoke
soup 112
smoked trout pâté 40
hot fruit salad 114

Lee Yuan
spiced spare ribs 30

Leith's
pigeon casserole with
celery and walnuts 49

Lockets
Lockets savoury 42
soft herring roes in white
wine sauce 139

Mon Plaisir
   stuffed shoulder of veal   26

Odin's
   Mrs Langan's chocolate
     pudding   76

Panos Restaurant
   chicken chanfaina   163

Rules
   steak and kidney
     pudding   89

Simple Simon
   potage de garbanzos   103

Tiberio
   agnello e patate alla Villa
     Cesare   46

White Tower
   moussaka   163

General Index

Agnello e patate alla Villa
   Cesare   46

Almond, almonds
   with apricot torte   61
   and celery soup   137
   and cherry tart   105
   gateau Fontes   42
   and watercress soup   20

Ambroisie de pêches   71

American
   cheesecake   81
   chicken salad   84

Angel pie   144

Apple
   cold curried soup   79
   and Stilton savoury   90
   tarte aux pommes
     Joséphine   95
   Waldorf salad   108

Apricot
   and ginger sauce with
     duck   138
   streusel   118
   torte with almonds   61

Armenian
   kishmish   27

Arnold Bennett, omelette   74

Arrowroot, for thickening
   sauces   169

Artichoke, and scallop
   soup   112

Asparagus
   flan   25
   tortilla mimosa   74

Avocado
   au gratin   147
   Highbullen's guacamole   160
   mousse   40
   mousse aux crevettes   142

Aubergines
   moussaka   163
   stuffed, au gratin   161

Australian
   raspberry Pavlova   66

Baie des Anges, sole   117

Bain-marie   168

Ballotine of duck   138

Basic recipes   168

Basil Brush, pork   113

Batter, for pancakes   172

Beaujolais and prune
   sauce   105

Beef
   braised in red wine   36
   carbonnade flamande   133
   moussaka   163
   steak à la moutarde   60
   steak and kidney
     pudding   89
   stock   170
   tournedos Médicis   60

Belle Anna, oeufs   45

Bell Inn smokies   88

Beurre manié   169

Beurre noisette, ris de
   veau au   99

Bisque, tuna and corn   20

Blackcurrant ice-cream   71

Bouquet garni   168

Bourgeoise, matelote   158

Braised beef in red wine   36

Bread
   brioche   167
   hot garlic   165
   wholemeal   166

Brioche   167

British
   apple and Stilton
     savoury   90
   Bell Inn smokies   88
   coddled pockets   128
   gooseberry meringue tart   66
   gosebery tarte   166
   kidneys in Madeira   153
   kipper pâté   152
   lemon syllabub   154
   Lockets savoury   42
   mackerel pâté   152
   marinated kipper fillets   88
   Mrs Langan's chocolate
     pudding   76
   omelette Arnold Bennett   74
   orange caramel trifle   32
   pork Basil Brush   113
   quick syllabub   154
   Sailors' Lament   22
   smoked haddock
     croquettes   64
   smoked trout pâté   40
   soft herring roes in
     white wine   139
   steak and kidney
     pudding   89
   sticky toffee pudding   165
   toasted savoury cheese   139
   venison pie   143

Brown beef stock   170

Brown bread ice-cream 37

Butter
  beurre manié 169
  beurre noisette 99
  clarified 168
  garlic 127

Butterscotch sauce 159

Cabbage
  with onion 36
  red 49

Campagne, terrine de 45

Canard, terrine de,
  aux raisins 157

Caneton aux olives 65

Caramel
  ice-cream 37
  orange trifle 32
  tarte aux pommes
    Joséphine 95

Carbonnade flamande 133

Casareccia, involtini alla 55

Casseroled
  pigeon with celery and
    walnuts 49
  pheasant 123

Celery
  and almond soup 137
  casserole, with pigeon
    and walnuts 49
  and orange salad 127
  Waldorf salad 108

Chachouka 54

Chanfaina, chicken 163

Charles Stuart, fraises 56

Charlotte, orange and
  lemon 50

Cheese
  apple and Stilton savoury 90
  cheesecake, American 81
  cheesecake, Italian 81
  crêpes gruyère 164
  Lockets savoury 42
  toasted savoury 139

Cheesecake
  American 81
  Italian 81

Cherry and almond tart 105

Chestnuts
  parfait au marron 129
  pureed with potato 101

Chicken
  American chicken salad 84
  chanfaina 163
  de Vaux 21
  poulet au gratin à la
    crème landaise 94
  stock 171

Chilled cream of
  mushroom soup 103

Chinese
  spiced spare ribs 30

Chocolate
  brandy cake 22
  cream with maraschino 109
  crème velour 109
  mint sauce 159
  mousse au chocolat 27
  Mrs Langan's chocolate
    pudding 76
  oranges in 124
  parfait au marron 129
  Sailors' Lament 22
  whisky gateau 149

Clarified butter 168

Cocktail, prawn 69

Coddled pockets 128

Coffee
  gateau Fontes 42

Cold
  curried apple soup 79
  Love 100

Coeur de filet de porc
  aux herbes 70

Coquilles St. Jacques,
  Hotel de la Poste 132

Corn and tuna bisque 20

Cornflour, for thickening
  sauces 169

Crab
  and fresh grapefruit
    salad 59
  mousse 69

Cream
  cauliflower soup 112
  chilled mushroom soup 103
  chocolate cream with
    maraschino 109
  crème velour 109
  leeks in 99
  mussels in curry sauce 122
  onion tart 25
  orange curd 84
  poulet au gratin à la
    crème landaise 94
  strawberry pots de crème 56

Crêpes
  basic recipe 172
  gruyère 164

Inwoods savoury
  pancakes 98
  sole Baie des Anges 117

Croquettes of smoked
  haddock 64

Cucumber
  and yoghourt salad 75
  iced soup 137

Curd cream, orange 84

Curry, curried
  cold apple soup 79
  sauce with marrow 90
  and cream sauce with
    mussels 122

Darne de saumon de
  Médicis 80

Double boiler 168

Drambuie
  flummery 129
  fraises Charles Stuart 56

Dubonnet and orange with
  liver 41

Duck
  ballotine 138
  caneton aux olives 65
  roast 162
  terrine de canard aux
    raisins 157

Duxelles 168

Eggs
  Chachouka 54
  oeufs à la neige 134
  oeufs Belle Anna 45
  omelette Arnold Bennett 74
  tortilla mimosa 74

Fasulya 75

Filets
  coeur de porc aux herbes 70
  de porc aux pruneaux   148

Fillets, marinated kipper 88

Fish
  Bell Inn smokies   88
  coquilles St Jacques   132
  crab mousse   69
  darne de saumon de
    Médicis   80
  fresh grapefruit and crab
    salad   59
  fresh herring pâté   160
  kipper pâté   152
  mackerel pâté   152
  marinated kipper fillets 88
  matelote bourgeoise   158
  moules marinière   122
  mussels in cream and
    curry sauce   122
  Pinks fish soup   161
  prawn cocktail   69
  salmon pâté   83
  scallop and artichoke
    soup   112
  scampi façon Gourmet   108
  smoked haddock
    croquettes   64
  smoked trout pâté   40
  soft herring roes in
    white wine   139
  sole Baie des Anges   117
  stuffed tomatoes   98
  tuna and corn bisque   20
  turbot kebabs with
    shrimp sauce   31

Flan (see also tarts)
  asparagus   25

Flan case, to line   173

Flummery Drambuie   129

Fontes, gateau   42
Fraises Charles Stuart   56
French
  blackcurrant ice-cream   71
  brioche   166
  caneton aux olives   65
  carbonnade flamande   133
  chocolate whisky
    gateau   149
  coeur de filet de porc
    aux herbes   70
  coquilles St. Jacques,
    Hotel de la Poste   132
  crêpes gruyère   164
  darne de saumon de
    Médicis   80
  dressing   172
  filets de porc
    aux pruneaux   148
  matelote bourgeoise   158
  moules marinière   122
  mousse au chocolat   27
  oeufs à la neige   134
  onion cream tart   25
  parfait au marron   129
  paysanne   26
  poulet au gratin à la
    crème landaise   94
  ratatouille   54
  ris de veau au beurre
    noisette   99
  salade niçoise   59
  sole Baie des Anges   117
  steak à la moutarde   60
  stuffed aubergine au
    gratin   161
  stuffed shoulder of veal 26
  tarte aux pommes
    Joséphine   95
  terrine de campagne   45
  terrine de canard aux
    raisins   157
  turbot kebabs with shrimp
    sauce   31

Fresh
  grapefruit and crab salad 59
  herring pâté   160

Fruit salad, hot   114

Game
  casseroled pheasant   123
  Jaegermeister pâté   108
  pigeon casserole   49
  venison pie   143

Garbanzos, potage de   103

Garlic
  hot bread   165
  mushrooms in butter   127

Gateau
  chocolate whisky   149
  Fontes   42

Gazpacho   64

German
  apricot streusel   118
  apricot torte with
    almonds   61
  Jaegermeister pâté   108

Gooseberries
  gosebery tarte   166
  meringue tart   66

Gourmet, scampi façon   108

Grapefruit and crab salad 59

Gratin, au
  avocado   147
  poulet à la crème
    landaise   94
  stuffed aubergines   161

Greek
  chicken chanfaina   163
  moussaka   163

Gruyère, crêpes   164

Guacamole, Highbullen's   160

Haddock, croquettes of
  smoked   64

Herring
  fresh in pâté   160
  soft roes in white wine 139

Highbullen's guacamole   160

Honey-baked spare ribs   30

Hot
  fruit salad   114
  garlic bread   165

Ice-cream
  blackcurrant   71
  brown bread   37
  butterscotch sauce for   159
  caramel   37
  mint chocolate sauce for 159
  peach Melba   114

Iced cucumber soup   137

Involtini alla casareccia 55

Inwoods savoury pancake   98

Italian
  agnello e patate alla Villa
    Cesare   46
  cheesecake   81
  involtini alla casereccia 55
  pignatelle   35

Jaegermeister pâté with
  Waldorf salad   108

Jeryik   75

Joséphine, tarte aux
  pommes   95

Kebabs, turbot with
shrimp sauce 31

Kidney, kidneys
in Madeira 153
and steak puddi ng 89

Kipper
marinated fillets 88
pâté 152

Kirsch, naranjas al 124

Kishmish 27

Lamb
agnello e patate alla
Villa Cesare 46
fasulya 75
moussaka 163

Landaise, poulet au gratin
à la crème 94

Lament, Sailors' 22

Leeks in cream 99

Lemon
and orange charlotte 50
soup 79
syllabub 154

Liver with Dubonnet and
orange 41

Lockets savoury 42

Love, Cold 100

Mackerel pâté 152

Madeira, kidneys in 153

Maraschino, with chocolate
cream 109

Marinated kpper fillets 88

Marron, parfait au 129

Marrow with curry sauce 90

Matelote bourgeoise 158

Mayonnaise 171

Médicis
darne de saumon de 80
tournedos 60

Melba, peach 114

Meringue
angel pie 144
and gooseberry tart 66
raspberry Pavlova 66

Mexican
Highbullen's guacamole 160

Mimosa, tortilla 74

Mint chocolate sauce 159

Moules marinière 122

Moussaka 163

Mousse
au chocolat 27
avocado 40
avocado aux crevettes 142
crab 69
Snaffles 142

Moutarde, steak à la 60

Mrs Langan's chocolate
pudding 76

Mushrooms
chilled cream soup 103
duxelles 168
in garlic butter 127
pickled 147

Mussels
moules marinière 122
in cream and curry
sauce 122

Naranjas al kirsch 124

Neige, oeufs à la 134

Niçoise, salade 59

Oak House pâté 83

Oeufs
à la neige 134
Belle Anna 45

Offal
kidneys in Madeira 153
liver with Dubonnet and
orange 41
Oak House pâté 83
ris de veau au beurre
noisette 99

Olives, caneton aux 65

Omelettes
Arnold Bennett 74
tortilla mimosa 74

Onion
with cabbage 36
cream tart 25

Orange, oranges
caramel trifle 32
and celery salad 127
in chocolate 124
curd cream 84
and lemon charlotte 50
naranjas al kirsch 124
and port sauce 104

Pancakes (see also crêpes) 172
basic recipe 98
Inwoods savoury

Parfait au marron 129

Pastry
choux 35
shortcrust 173
Vienna 61

Patate e agnello alla Villa
Cesare 46

Pâtés (see also terrines)
fresh herring 160
Jaegermeister 108
kipper 152
mackerel 152
Oak House 83
salmon 83
smoked trout 40

Pavlova, raspberry 66

Paysanne 26

Peach, peaches
ambroisie de pêches 71
Melba 114

Pears
Lockets savoury 42
spiced 47

Pheasant, casseroled 123

Pickled
mushrooms 147
pineapple 104

Pigeon casserole with celery
and walnuts 49

Pignatelle (pine cones) 35
Pilaff 174
Pineapple, pickled 104
Pinks fish soup 161
Pockets, coddled 128
Pommes
  parisienne 163
  tarte Joséphine 95
Pork
  Basil Brush 113
  coeur de filets aux herbes 70
  filets aux pruneaux 148
  spare ribs in honey 30
  spiced spare ribs 30
Port and orange sauce 104
Potage de garbanzos 103
Potatoes
  patate alla Villa Cesare 46
  pommes parisienne 163
  pureed with chestnuts 101
  rösti 113
Pots de crème, strawberry 56
Poulet au gratin à la
  crème landaise 94
Prawns
  cocktail 69
  scampi façon Gourmet 108
Prunes
  and Beaujolais sauce 105
  filet de porc aux
    pruneaux 148
Pudding
  steak and kidney 89
  sticky toffee 165

Quick syllabub 154
Raspberry Pavlova 66
Ratatouille 54
Red cabbage 49
Red wine, braised beef in 36
Reduction, to thicken
  sauces 170
Rice, pilaff 174
Ris de veau au beurre
  noisette 99
Roast duck 162
Roes, soft herring, in
white wine 139
Rösti 113
Roux 169
Rum
  Cold Love 100
  Sailors' Lament 22
Sailors' Lament 22
Salade niçoise 59
Salads
  American chicken 84
  cucumber and yoghort 75
  grapefruit and crab 59
  hot fruit 114
  orange and celery 127
  salade niçoise 59
  Waldorf 108
Salmon
  darne de Médicis 80
  pâté 83
  stuffed tomatoes 98

Sauces
  béarnaise 174
  béchamel 174
  butterscotch with
    ice-cream 159
  demi-glace 172
  mayonnaise 171
  mint chocolate with
    ice-cream 159
  port and orange with
    duck 104
  prune and Beaujolais
    with duck 105
  shrimp with turbot 31
  tartare 171
  to thicken 169–170
Savouries
  Lockets 42
  soft herring roes in
    white wine 139
  Stilton and apple 90
  toasted cheese 139
Scallops
  and artichoke soup 112
  coquilles St. Jacques,
    Hotel de la Poste 132
Scampi façon Gourmet 108
Shortcrust pastry
  plain 173
  rich 173
  sweet 173
Shoulder of veal, stuffed 26
Shrimp, shrimps
  with avocado mousse 142
  oeufs Belle Anna 45
  sauce with turbot 31
Smoked
  haddock croquettes 64
  trout pâté 40
Smokies, Bell Inn 88

Snaffles mousse 142
Soft herring roes in white
  wine 139
Sole Baie des Anges 117
Soups
  almond and watercress
    (cold) 20
  celery and almond 137
  chilled cream of
    mushroom 103
  cold curried apple 79
  cream of cauliflower 112
  gazpacho (cold) 64
  iced cucumber 137
  lemon 79
  Pinks fish 161
  potage de garbanzos 103
  scallop and artichoke 112
  spinach 93
  tomato 93
  tuna and corn bisque 20
Spanish
  Cold Love 100
  gazpacho 64
  naranjas al kirsch 124
  potage de garbanzos 103
  tortilla mimosa 74
Spare ribs
  in honey 30
  spiced 30
Spiced
  pears 47
  spare ribs 30
Spinach
  Inwoods savoury pancake 98
  soup 93
Spun sugar 134

Steak
  and kidney pudding 89
  à la moutarde 60
  tournedos Médicis 60

Sticky toffee pudding 165

Stilton and apple savoury 90

Stock
  brown beef 170
  chicken 171
  fish 117

Strawberries
  fraises Charles Stuart 56
  pots de crème 56

Streusel, apricot 118

Stuffed
  aubergines au gratin 161
  shoulder of veal 26
  tomatoes 98

Sugar
  spun 134
  vanilla 169

Sweetbreads
  ris de veau au beurre
    noisette 99

Swiss
  rösti 113

Syllabub
  lemon 154
  quick 154

Tartare sauce 171

Tarte aux pommes
  Joséphine 95

Tarte, gosebery 166

Tarts
  asparagus flan 25
  cherry and almond 105

gooseberry meringue 66
onion cream 25
tarte aux pommes
  Joséphine 95

Terrines (see also pâtés)
  de campagne 45
  de canard aux raisins 157

Thickening agents 169–170

Toasted savoury cheese 139

Tomato, tomatoes
  gazpacho 64
  soup 93
  stuffed 98
  tomates provençale 70

Torte, apricot with
  almonds 61

Tortilla mimosa 74

Tournedos Médicis 60

Trifle, orange caramel 32

Trout, smoked in pâté 40

Tuna
  and corn bisque 20
  salade niçoise 59
  stuffed tomatoes 98

Tunisian 54
  chachouka

Turbot kebabs with
  shrimp sauce 31

Turkish
  fasulya 75
  jeryik 75

Vanilla sugar 169

Vaux, chicken de 21

Veal
  coddled pockets 128
  involtini alla casareccia 55
  stuffed shoulder 26

Vegetables
  cabbage with onion 36
  leeks in cream 99
  marrow in curry sauce 90
  patate alla Villa Cesare 46
  paysanne 26
  pommes parisienne 163
  ratatouille 54
  red cabbage 49
  rösti 113
  tomates provençale 70

Velour, crème 109

Venison
  Jaegermeister pâté 108
  pie 143

Vienna pastry 61

Vinaigrette 172

Waldorf salad 108

Walnuts, pigeon and celery
  casserole 49

Watercress
  and almond soup 20
  Lockets savoury 42

White wine, soft herring
  roes in 139

Wholemeal bread 166

Yoghourt and cucumber
  salad 75

Index of wines

Australia
Coonawarra (red) 126

Austria
Riesling 73

Bulgaria
Gamza (red) 39
Melnik (red) 73
Cabernet (red) 73

Chile
Claret (red) 63

France
Alsace
Gewürztraminer
  39, 136, 151
Pinot Gris (Tokay d'Alsace) 92
Riesling 19, 151
Traminer 63
Beaujolais 102, 111, 156
Fleurie 44, 102
Morgon 102, 111
Moulin-à-Vent 111
Bordeaux
red (*claret*)
Côte de Bourg 126
Fronsac 126
Margaux
  Ch. Palmer 44
St-Estèphe 58
  Ch. Cos d'Estournel 58
  Ch. Montrose 44
St Emilion 58, 97, 151
  Ch. Figeac 97
  Ch. Gaffelière-Naudes 97
  Ch. Pavie 58
St Julien

Ch. Léoville Las-Cases 44
Pomerol
  Ch. l'Evangile 97
  Ch. La Fleur Pourret 97
white
Barsac
  Ch. Climens 58
  Ch. Coutet 58
  Cérons 29
  Loupiac 29
Sauternes
  Ch. d'Yquem 29
Burgundy
Aligoté (white) 24
Chablis 131
  Les Clos 131
  Fourchaume 131

Côte de Beaune: 48
red
  Beaune 48, 87
  Pommard 48, 87
  Volnay 48, 146
  Volnay-Caillerets 58
white
  Chassagne-Montrachet 29
  Corton-Charlemagne 78
  Mâcon-Viré 44
  Meursault 29, 78, 107
  Puligny-Montrachet 107

Côte de Nuits:
red
  Morey-St-Denis 151
  Nuits-St-Georges 102, 141
  Vosne-Romanée 141
  Vosne-Suchots 58
white
  Mâcon
  Pouilly-Fuissé 131, 146
Mercurey
  Montagny (white) 131
Champagne 116
Dordogne
Monbazillac 116

Graves
 red
Ch. Haut-Bailly 92
Ch. Pape-Clément 92
Ch. La-Mission-Haut-
  Brion 92
 white
Ch. Laville-Haut-Brion 73
Ch. Olivier 73
Loire and Anjou
Anjou 116
  Coteaux du Layon 116
  rosé 19
Muscadet 121
Pouilly-Fumé 24
Sancerre 121
Saumur (sparkling) 82
Touraine
  Chinon 39
  Bourgeuil 24, 39
Vouvray 78
Provence
Bandol 63
Rhône
Châteauneuf-du-Pape
 red 121, 131
Côte Rôtie 68, 121
Gigondas 131
Hermitage
 red 68
 white 48, 156
Vermouth
Chambéry 39, 156
dry white 63

Germany
Rhine
Nahe
  Schloss Böckelheimer 97
  Kreuznacher 29
  Rüdesheimer 107
Palatinate
  Dürkheimer 97
Rheingau
  Johannisberger 29
Rheinhesse
  Niersteiner 102
  Oppenheimer 102
Moselle
Bernkasteler 82
Graacher 82

Hungary
Riesling 73
  white 44

Italy
Asti Spumante 58
Bardolino 126
Barolo 34, 102, 141
Chianti Classico 53, 126
Grignolino 126
Soave 44
Valpolicella 24, 111

Madeira
  Bual 87
  Sercial 136
  Verdelho 87

Pilsner 121

Portugal
Dão (red) 131
Port
  late bottled 87, 136
  white 136, 156
rosé 19
vinho verde 82

Rumania
  Cabernet (red) 39

Spain
Rioja 34, 53, 136
Sherry
  Amontillado 87
  fino 29, 34, 63
  Manzanilla 29
  Montilla 34
  Oloroso 87

Switzerland
Chablais 107

Turkey
Buzbag (red) 73

United Kingdom
malt whisky 87
Guinness 87
barley wine 87
cider (dry) 87